Teacher and Pupil

STUDENTS LIBRARY OF EDUCATION

d are ultimately educational in nature and there-
go beyond the confines of any supposed value-free
ce. Students and teachers are invited to look at their
ls and themselves in terms which make clear the
onal context in which education takes place.

BEN MORRIS

Teacher and Pupil

Some Socio-Psychological Aspects

Philip Gammage
School of Education
University of Bristol

London
Routledge & Kegan Paul

First published 1971
by Routledge & Kegan Paul Ltd
Broadway House
68-74 Carter Lane
London EC4V 5EL
Printed in Great Britain by
Northumberland Press Ltd

ISBN 0 7100 7135 3 (c)
0 7100 7136 1 (p)

THE STUDENTS LIBRARY OF E1
designed to meet the needs of Stud
Colleges of Education and at Univ
Departments. It will also be valu
teachers and educationists. The seri
of the latest developments in teac
new methods and approaches in e
volumes will provide authoritati
accounts of the topics within the m
logy, philosophy and history of edu
psychology, and method. Care has
specialist topics are treated lucidly a1
non-specialist reader. Altogether, the
of Education will provide a comprehe
and guide to anyone concerned with t
tion, and with educational theory and

cuss
fore
scie1
pup
pers

One aspect of the current trend toward:
alization of teaching is the increasing em
science disciplines as relevant fields o
initial and inservice education of t
psychology in particular is seen as bein
portance in the understanding of the tea
of pupil-teacher interaction. There can
that one of the most effective approache
psychology of education is through suc
Gammage's book deals with these and sim
direct practical concern to teachers. It i
pave the way for more systematic study
while at the same time making it clear that

Contents

CONTENTS

Preface

Within the last hundred years or so western societies have devised pervasive and powerful institutions which have a radical and moulding effect upon children, almost equal to that of the family. All must attend such institutions in one form or another and many spend at least half their waking life in attendance prior to adulthood. The only comparable institutions of such compulsion are prisons.

The common myth that is perpetuated seems to be one of schooldays being the happiest days of one's life. Many children to whom I have spoken are neither so complacent nor so romantic. For many of them still, school represents coercion and the squandering of their time on tasks of little apparent relevance to their lives. For many others it represents an authority over-mindful of its position and ever ready to instil in the growing person a sense of academic inadequacy – a consciousness of inappropriate linguistic style or a sense of rejection by 'them'. Whilst undoubtedly many teachers are sensitive and dedicated to the enrichment of child-

ren's lives, many are not; and many other adults see
the school as not only an important agent of socialization, but as an agent for maintaining the *status quo* and
not one permitted to allow for the dynamics of change.

This is not to say that teachers are themselves always
resistant to change. Quite often the reverse is true, and
they act as powerful pressure groups capable of promoting educational and social change. For instance, whilst
in Michigan, U.S.A., in 1969 I observed much contro-
versy over the devising of sex-education programmes
for the State's schools. The impetus for these programmes came mainly from the teachers, but many of
the parents (and notably the John Birch Society) were
actively opposed to any sex-education and were con-
ducting an opposing campaign with considerable vehe-
mence. But equally, it must be remembered that
teachers by virtue of their occupation and training may
well assimilate and represent views that are static and
overtly middle class.

In England most of the work written about schools as
institutions has been by sociologists rather than social
psychologists and there has been relatively little work
(outside the U.S.A.) as yet concerned with group psychology within the classroom, or the role of the teacher.
Notable exceptions are studies by Fleming (1959),
Morris (1965) and Richardson (1967). There is, however,
considerably more work of a psycho-analytically orientated nature into group behaviour and learning, such as
that influential book of W. R. Bion's, *Experience in
Groups* (1963), and in the last few years some reviving
of interest in the teacher's role (Hoyle, 1969 and Musgrove and Taylor, 1969). The work of the Americans
Rosenthal and Jacobsen in 1968, though condemned by

some for inexpertise in research technique, nevertheless fostered new interest in the school class and the expectations of the teacher; and work in England by Bernstein, Lawton, Barnes and others is concentrating ever more attention upon inadequacies and differences in language styles.

The social psychology of learning is still in its infancy, particularly if compared with the psychology of learning. The fact that school learning takes place in a social context – a context of socialization of a certain sort – and the fact that such learning is to a large part affected by the learner's attitudes to the content and context of his learning, are both causing more attention to be focused upon the formal and informal structures of school organization. Yet these attitudes are often integral to processes rooted in our childhood, in the individual's personality system and within the groupings and affiliations of school life. Any consideration, therefore, of institutionalized mass education is incomplete if it ignores the nature of group processes and their interweaving with cognitive development.

This book is an attempt to outline some of the major points pertinent to the study of the school class as a group and to the formation of some of the attitudes of the children and teacher as they relate to education.

1
The elements of
group dynamics

Historical background: milestones in the study of inter-action

The functioning of any complex society depends upon both casual and institutionalized interaction to a large degree, and inevitably elements of codes, norms and roles enter into such relationships. Much of this interaction takes place in fairly small face-to-face groups gathered together for some specific purpose. Group dynamics constitute the study of adjustive changes in the group and the change in structure of any part of the group. But in actual fact the term is used much more loosely to cover the study of small groups generally.

In 1909 C. H. Cooley put forward the argument that certain groups of people could be termed 'primary' in nature since they occurred almost universally. At about the same time Emile Durkheim in France was working on the importance of the group in human behaviour and Georg Simmel in Germany writing on interaction processes. There is little doubt that these three directly influenced the thinking of the philosopher and student of human behaviour, George Herbert Mead. Mead was concerned to show that man is a social animal and that it is the primary group which is predominantly responsible for the training of the individual and for providing him with a seed-bed for his psychological development. Mead published little before his death in 1931 but had a great influence on his students at the University of Chicago – many of whom have regarded him as the father of social psychology.

Freud, too, had certainly given a great deal of thought to the development of the child within the primary group and it is fair to say that modern psychoanalytic group therapy owes much to Freud's speculative writings published in his *Group Psychology and the Analysis of the Ego* (1921). In this book Freud speaks of the importance of the influence of the group leader and the way in which the group is held together by identification with the leader.

In Cooley's terms primary groups were defined as groups which exhibited feelings of unity or solidarity, which operated in face-to-face relationships and which produced, mirrored and reinforced the social and moral normative expectations of an adult society. Usually, the family is considered to be a 'primary group'. But so might be the school gang, a college club or a fraternity, or the play group or village. Generally, there are motives and incentives which cause group members to remain group members, and additional motives for belonging tend to result from the interaction itself.

After some popularity Cooley's theory was disregarded for many years (Faris, 1937) and much more attention paid to the so-called 'secondary groups' (i.e.

groups characterized by contractual relationship rather than primary relationship). Secondary groups are considered to be those larger social aggregates such as trade unions, learned societies, social classes, or religious denominations, which, whilst often possessing explicit written codes and rules for behaviour, are too unwieldy or too amorphous to act with the same intimate pervasiveness.

Increasingly, however, from the 1940s onwards more sociologists and social psychologists appear to have rediscovered what early cultural psychoanalysts (such as Harry Stack Sullivan and Trigant Burrow) had taken as central to much of their work: the importance of the primary agents of socialization. In fact the Second World War acted as a catalyst to the study of group dynamics. Factors like morale, the efficiency of the troops and subordinate relationships tended to come under closer scrutiny in order to maximize the effectiveness of the war effort (see the work of Stouffer *et al.*, 1949). Also, much of the research in linguistics, psycholinguistics and socio-linguistics, particularly in the U.S.A., seems to have its roots in the work of social psychologists studying communication, attitude formation, rumour, role-playing and gang life. Indeed, many social psychologists regard language as the keystone to the study of the individual in society.

Particularly prominent in the study of group dynamics have been Lewin and his former students Lippitt and White. Kurt Lewin, a German Gestalt psychologist originally, who died in 1947, was largely responsible for a revival in interest in children's social behaviour. He worked at Cornell and then at the University of Michigan. He was in large measure responsible for the establishment of the Research Center for Group Dynamics at the University of Michigan. This centre has helped to make the university pre-eminent in the field of social psychology. Probably Lewin's most famous generalization is that on the whole it is easier to change an individual's behaviour when he is a member of a group than when he is separate and alone.

In 1938 *An Experimental Approach to the Study of Autocracy and Democracy* was published and in 1939 the results of the work with R. K. White on leadership in children's groups became available. Lewin and his associates were also probably the first to study the effect of group decisions upon individual behaviour and attitudes (in the late 1940s and early 1950s). At about the same time R. F. Bales (1951) was developing his now famous system which he termed 'an interaction process analysis'. He attempted to conceptualize social interaction in terms of a problem-solving sequence, and there is little doubt that, though a classic preliminary investigation, his categories are over-generalized. Bales attempted to devise a classificatory system which could be used to study the interaction of any group regardless of its background history and composition. Each of his categories places heavy emphasis on verbal communication, and the non-verbal aspects are probably not given sufficient weight (the unit of observation to be 'the smallest discriminable segment of verbal or non-verbal behaviour' – Bales, 1951). Bales suggests that each category can be taken to constitute a dimension exclusive of others. Thus, the observer would be able to place the observable behaviour of any group member into one of the following categories:

Categories used in the Bales Category System (adapted)

A   The emotionally positive responses
   1 Shows solidarity
   2 Shows tension release
   3 Agrees

B   Problem-solving responses (answers)
   4 Gives suggestions
   5 Gives opinions
   6 Gives orientation

C   Problem-solving responses (questions)
   7 Asks for orientation
   8 Asks for opinions
   9 Asks for suggestions

D   Emotionally negative responses
   10 Disagrees
   11 Shows tension
   12 Shows antagonism

The Bales system provides for scoring and profiles that can be used for comparative analysis of group functioning. In addition to the profile of general group structure, the observer also identifies each member and recipient during the process. Besides the Bales system there are several others in use (such as that of Carter *et al.*, 1951) and there is also much work in the field of participant observation (such as that stemming from Whyte, 1943).

H. J. Leavitt, L. S. Christie, R. B. Luce and J. Macy considerably furthered the work of task communication and performance in small groups in the early 1950s.

These studies showed that different degrees of efficiency in solution were related to both the nature of the task and the type of communication structure employed. Indeed, the main topics of concern to students of group dynamics seem to be those of communication and sentiment. Homans says (1951), 'When we make a statement about the mutual dependence of, for instance, interaction and activity, we must never forget that sentiment also comes into the system and may affect the relationships described.'

Foremost in the study of group dynamics has been the University of Michigan, Ann Arbor, U.S.A., and much of the impetus for the study of group dynamics in relation to educational psychology derives from the work of Alvin F. Zander and others (see particularly Trow *et al.*, 1950). But small-group theory is useful not only in the study of education; it is of particular use in such fields as counselling, psychotherapy, business administration and social work generally. Very readable introductions exist in Josephine Klein's *The Study of Groups* (1956) and W. J. H. Sprott's *Human Groups* (1958) and a great deal of relevant material may be found in *Readings in Social Psychology* edited by Newcomb and Hartley in 1947 and in subsequent volumes by Maccoby, Newcomb and Hartley; *Group Dynamics* edited by Cartwright and Zander (1955) and *Social Psychology* by Secord and Backman (1964).

Dyadic relationships and communication

A useful starting point for the study of interaction is to take the simplest unit of sociological analysis, which is that of a pair of individuals influencing each other within a given social context. Georg Simmel (1858-1918) appears to have been the first to stress the importance of interaction. Indeed, his work is reputed to have had considerable influence on American sociology (though sociology is, of course, not merely or only concerned with interaction *per se*, but with the fact that the inter-action is affected by the social structure within which it takes place. It therefore of necessity involves norms, status positions and obligations). This 'interaction of self and other is the most elementary form of social system' (Parsons and Shils, 1952) and present in more complex forms in all social systems.

In interaction ego and alter are each objects of orientation for the other. The basic differences from orientations to non-social objects are two. First, since the outcome of ego's action (e.g. success in the attainment of a goal) is contingent on alter's reaction to what ego does, ego becomes orientated not only to alter's probable overt behaviour but also to what ego interprets to be alter's expectations relative to ego's behaviour, since ego expects that alter's ex-pectations will influence alter's behaviour. Second, in an integrated system, this orientation to the expecta-tions of the other is reciprocal or complementary.

Parsons and Shils maintain that this orientation is reciprocated not only in the relationship of two people (dyadic behaviour) but multiply reciprocated at differ-ent levels in small groups. Various methods of study can be employed to ascertain the perceptions made and expectations held by ego for alter (see in particular Cronbach, 1961).

Obviously, if one is to measure expectations and to reciprocate even at the level of dyadic behaviour, there must normally be some common code or system of symbols which is mutually accessible. Generalizations will have been made – often based on prior experience and normative assumptions. As Parsons and Shils point out, when such generalization has occurred and it is apparent that 'actions, gestures or symbols have more or less the *same* meaning for both ego and alter [then] we may speak of a common culture existing between them, through which their interaction is mediated'. Another aspect of this is that the meaning of any communication from one person to another is to a large extent dependent upon the degree to which that communication fits into the recipient's cognitive structure. Thus communication becomes a sort of 'guessing game'. 'Each person carries with him his cognitive field as a map of the world. He responds not to the world but to the map. When he receives a communication, the meaning it has is a consequence of how it can be fitted into the map' (Runkel, 1956). In this theory accurate communication depends not on passing 'packets of information' but on the degree to which the cognitive maps of the communicators can be deemed similar. The interesting thing about both viewpoints quoted is that they point to an 'appropriate' set of expectations being built up in such a way that a number of appropriate reactions and complementary expectations form a normative pattern. The cultural habitat of even a dyadic relationship is not only a set of symbols of communication, but a set of norms for action. Put simply, you behave to some extent in the way you *think* other people feel is appropriate for you – and this behaviour tends to act as a conditioning factor upon their expectations and attitudes which they may well in turn modify in the light of your subsequent behaviour and which

8

will in turn modify your attitudes towards them. Eventually some sort of equilibrium of expectations tends to exist in a given context.

Primary groups: leadership, conformity and cohesion

Passing from dyadic interaction to primary groups, it is as well to remember that in the larger situation, too, these members are not linked by 'contractual obligation', but by shared loyalties or common beliefs. In such groups relationships tend to be personal and intimate. Whilst family and friendship groups are obvious examples, informal spontaneous primary groups can also function, i.e. at a large party, at a conference, or a temporary community of some sort. 'Primary groups obviously share many of the characteristics of a communal society' and are *primary* in the sense that they can be found in all sorts of societies'. Much more important, 'they provide the most significant social and psychological context for individual experience' (Chinoy, 1954).

Within the confines of the primary group the child acquires much that is basic to his personality. This perception of others and their roles is of vital importance (see, for instance, the work of psychoanalysts on the importance of object relationships and particularly the work of Bowlby *et al.*, 1966); yet much of this learning is not quantifiable since primary groups tend to operate informally and themselves 'grow' through the interaction, during which time regular patterns of behaviour and a sense of unity develop. Chinoy points out that such groups spring up wherever men and women meet together frequently – when children and friends play together, and in the midst of more highly organized groups in factories, offices, schools, etc. Furthermore, 'without formal organization of any sort (and sometimes even as a reaction against formal organization) a structure of interrelated roles and statuses comes into being, based upon shared beliefs and values.'

We tend in thinking of small groups to concentrate upon the fact that the group usually consists of members who are behaving alike in certain respects. Indeed, we often use words like gang or clique to summarize their important effects in a somewhat denigratory way. But groups do not merely have identifiable interest in common – or cohesiveness and insulation from outside. One of the positive potentials in any group, as most psychotherapists are aware, is that group awareness and self-awareness (particularly the second) depend upon the perception of individual differences and in part on the sensitive adjustment of these differences. (This might of course be countered by instances of groups that have coerced one or more of their members in such a way as to attempt an eradication of individual differences; it is necessary to stress both sides of the story.)

Generally there is a good deal of evidence to show that conformity is a tendency of people in groups. Abercrombie (1960) says, 'People prefer to be with those like themselves and, having chosen their companions, become even more alike.' Illustration of this may be found in an article by Newcomb (1960). His survey of interpersonal attraction dealt with a study of the behaviour of a group of seventeen men who lived together in a student's house for a year. It was found that long-lasting friendships were built on similarities and, rather than change attitudes, dissimilar people tended to break relationships. Furthermore, as time went by friends became more similar, particularly in their judgement of others. In respect of conformity of judgement S. E. Asch (1960) conducted a useful experiment in which a group of eight people were asked to match one line with three unequal others. Seven of the people were stooges and they unanimously contradicted the 'subject'. One third of the 'subjects' made errors echoing the opinions of the stooges.

In a book of readings by Cartwright and Zander (1960), Festinger and Aronsen contribute an article in which they say: 'The simultaneous existence of cognitions which one way or another do not fit together (i.e. are dissonant) leads to an effort on the part of the person to somehow make them fit better.' This dissonance reduction is very important since it tends to happen quite a lot in groups. (It is fairly common indeed to hear of school or service groups in which friends had originally held widely divergent views and had first been enemies.) It is important to remember that social interaction almost invariably involves some dissonance and often some disagreement with people like oneself. The degree of dissonance may well depend upon (a) the importance of the issue to the individual(s) concerned, and (b) the importance of the individual expressing the opposite view. You may, of course, convince yourself that the person disagreeing with you is unimportant, or that the issue itself is unimportant; or you may seek to change the other person's opinion and in this last you will probably tend to seek the support of others.

Conforming to the group depends to some extent upon the person's personality (which to a *limited* extent depends upon the group again). It is interesting to note that some psychologists hold the view that non-

conformers function better intellectually than conformers, and tend to be 'more confident, less rigid, less
authoritarian, more objective and realistic about their
parents and more permissive in their attitudes to child-
rearing practices' (Crutchfield, 1955). But these things
of themselves are to some extent dependent upon the
group climate.

White and Lippitt, in one of their classic experiments, showed that children behaved differently according to whether their clubs had an autocratic, democratic
or *laisser-faire* climate. (Leaders of the groups had been
specifically trained to establish such behaviour within
the group.) Every six weeks the leaders moved from one
club to another and changed their leadership style as
they did so. Thus each club, consisting of ten-year-old
boys roughly equated for intellectual, physical, personality and socio-economic factors, experienced three different climates under different leaders. Records were
kept of the behaviour of the leaders and boys during
each meeting.

Those leaders who took the autocratic role tended to
give orders, make disruptive commands interrupting
the boys' activities, and to be non-objective in giving
criticism and praise. On the other hand, those adopting
the other roles tended to control the boys by giving
information and making suggestions. The main difference between democratic and *laisser-faire* leadership
was reflected in the amount of guidance given when
deemed necessary. The democratic leaders were more
sensitive to the boys' welfare and participated more
fully in the life of the group than did the *laisser-faire*
leaders. Each leader reflected remarkable similarity
when playing similar roles. They tended to resemble

the role pattern rather than 'themselves'. To summarize:

1. Work done (painting, plastering, craftwork) was greatest in autocratic climates and least in *laisserfaire*, BUT
2. Motivation to work seemed greatest in the democratic climates because the boys tended to go on working even when the leader had left the room.
3. Work-orientated conversation was greatest in the democratic climates and least in *laisser-faire*
4. Nineteen out of twenty boys preferred democratic leaders
5. Most discontent was under autocracy (four of the boys who dropped out did so under autocratic regimes)
6. In autocratic climates the boys were most dependent and submissive yet were much more aggressive to each other
7. There was more originality, group-mindedness and friendly playfulness under democracy and more readiness to share.

It would perhaps be foolish to transfer the implications of this now rather elderly research straight into the classroom situation. This was an experiment deliberately set up. In less controlled conditions innumerable factors would be involved. In Deutsch's co-operation and competition experiment (Deutsch, 1960) psychology students were given puzzles and human relation problems to work at in discussion groups. The 'co-operative' groups were told that the grade obtained by each individual would depend upon the overall performance of the group. The 'competitive' groups were

13

told that each student would receive a grade related to his own contribution. As regards involvement or learning, very little difference could be observed between the two kinds of groups. But the 'co-operative' groups, when compared with the 'competitive' ones, had greater productivity per unit of time, a better quality of product and discussion, greater co-ordination of effort, more diversity in amount of contributions per member and more friendliness and careful listening to their fellows. Presumably, the main aim of a classroom group is the facilitation of learning. Such experiments as the above suggest that a democratic arrangement does help further efficient communication, considerable interaction and a happier atmosphere; not points to be lightly dismissed in favour of crudely quantitative measures of knowledge gained. 'The superiority of a climate of democratically guided participation over other climates, as regards solidarity, learning and productivity, is now generally accepted' (Morris, 1965).

But how does a group learn to function coherently and cohesively? First, it is useful to bear in mind that people conjoin for a purpose. Second, they usually have reasons for belonging; and third, the group involves its members in some interaction during the pursuance of its activities. Morris considers that 'In a group which has learned to work together effectively, we may pre-suppose both a common purpose and a high degree of member participation. But the appeal of a common purpose and the degree of member participation depend primarily on the inter-personal relations ('interactions' in behaviourist language) of the group members.' He places the related research in three broad categories:

1. Sociometric studies and psycho- and socio-drama
2. The work of Lewin and others in the U.S.A. (particularly the University of Michigan, Ann Arbor)
3. The psychoanalytically orientated work of W. R. Bion and others

and enters a useful caveat to the effect that, notwithstanding the extreme usefulness of such work, 'all three have been and are beset by dangers of over-elaboration and uncontrolled enthusiasm.' Whatever theories are adopted or exploited, the basic 'facts' of classroom application seem these. Many teachers treat group work as the answer to all learning problems. Much remains to be learned about the creation of good learning situations at all age levels. More classroom research is needed and this together with past research and its implications deserves to command more of the student-teacher's time.

If the school class as a group or the group within the class is to achieve something worthwhile, the tasks must be clearly delineated and at least in part actively desired or specified by the members themselves. The teacher, or 'opinion leader', to use Floud's term (Floud, 1962), must be sufficiently self-aware and secure to be able to accept difficulties, criticism and sometimes hostility. Such a leader must be ready to accept contributions from any source and to encourage all to contribute. He must know when to stand aside and not 'short-circuit' learning situations and he must know how to be involved and concerned without clouding his judgement. Lastly, he must be aware that in part the dynamics of good leadership depend upon his own ego-strength and self-concept. The institutionalized group leader is not well placed for a display of his own personal inadequacies.

2

Sociometry in the classroom

Moreno and Sociometry

Jacob L. Moreno, an émigré Austrian who settled in the U.S.A., is credited with being the first to use the term 'sociometry'. In the States Moreno based a small-group therapeutic and research technique on his earlier experiences as a refugee-camp administrator after the First World War. Moreno first expounded some of his ideas for the release of tension and the encouragement of spontaneity in a book called *Who Shall Survive?* published in the early thirties. But it was really left to others such as Jennings (1943) and Northway (1953) to utilize and systematize Moreno's early ideas for the detailed study of specific group situations. Helen Jennings did in fact work with Moreno and published much of her work in conjunction with him. Moreno was also responsible for the founding of a now well-known international journal, *Sociometry*, which is published under the auspices of the American Psychological Association. The practice of sociometry is the application of a technique for studying to whom an individual reaches out. For Moreno, it directly related to his theories on role-playing and the understanding and capacity of one person to perceive another's role. Though the techniques of sociometry are now quite widely taught in the States and used in the training and practice of counsellors as well as the training of teachers, there is little doubt that over the years there has been a tendency for Moreno's work to be somewhat denigrated as partisan. A pity, since there can be no denying his contributions to group psychology.

'The practice of sociometry consists of the administration of a questionnaire in which the subject chooses five other people in rank order of their attractiveness as associates.... It was later extended to cover negative choices. The results are plotted on paper in diagrammatic form, hence the term sociogram' (Duncan Mitchell, 1968).

What are its uses in the classroom? It can make explicit some of the more important and interesting relationships within the classroom as a whole, and it often helps to focus the teacher's attention upon isolates, particularly those isolates who are unobtrusive and submissive yet perform tolerably well in learning situations. One should, however, always be aware of the shifting and impermanent attitudes of the very young towards each other and of the fluidity of much early friendship.

Construction of classroom sociograms

To construct a sociogram one would normally wish to find out whom each child would choose to sit near, play with, or work with. Obviously, other activities could be substituted, but it is better to avoid extremely transitory activities. Remember that young children may find it very difficult to go beyond one choice. The choices of older children are often much more situationally specific and it may be necessary to specify several situations and then to compare the results. Furthermore, the children will need to have confidence in the teacher's fairness and sense of secrecy. They will not want their choices broadcast to all; and there is little point in carrying out a sociometric study if the teacher does not make use of the information gained for the planning of class seating, work-groups, etc. After making a simple chart for the classification of the choices, various types of sociogram can be constructed. Probably the most well-known and commonest used is the 'target' sociogram. This is simply a chart in the form of a target with the rings representing quartiles (or other proportions) of popularity. The most often chosen is situated centrally, the most infrequent (or the isolate) placed on the periphery. Relative positions may then be charted in between and can be seen at a glance. Different symbols can be used to represent boys or girls or different age levels. For a detailed explanation it would be well worthwhile reading M. L. Northway's *A Primer of Sociometry*.

Sociograms do not answer questions about the class as a group, they tend to pose them. Why are there certain members of high popularity? Why are the social isolates not chosen? Why are there clearly separated groups within larger groups? What are the value climates of these groups? Wisely used, the technique can certainly help the class teacher to become more perceptive of the children he teaches. In practice, particularly with older children of, say, the middle junior years and above, carefully administered sociometric tests make explicit (to the teacher) choices that really are consistent from week to week, especially for extremes. Frequently one is concerned to draw the isolate closer into the group, but one should not neglect to consider popular children as well. There is some evidence to suggest that the popular child is likely to be of above-average intelligence (Dentler and Mackler, 1962) and less dependent upon adults (McCandless *et al.*, 1961).

The greater the number of pupils and choices, the more complicated the sociogram becomes. A sociogram set out for a class of thirty to forty children would be likely to be fairly complex, unless it happened to resolve itself simply into a few relatively separate clusters. On the other hand, it is precisely with those larger groups that graphic portrayal becomes so useful and the teacher may well learn much more about the class than would have otherwise been apparent.

Amongst older children there are more or less stable patterns of interaction in the classroom. This does not imply that there will necessarily be unity. There may be a pattern which reflects several sub-groups loosely joined – or even several sub-groups which are mutually hostile. It is, however, extremely important for the teacher to pay attention to the nature of the class structure, since it will have some considerable bearing on the type of relationships which it is possible for the teacher to establish with the children. It will also reflect some of the problems which he is likely to meet.

One of the more useful aspects of sociometry in the classroom is the way that it can serve to underline, illustrate, or draw attention to the general ethos of the classroom and of its sub-groups. Who, for instance, are the high-status members? Is it the group with norms opposed to attainment and school work generally, or is it those who have popularity amongst the staff and above-average academic achievement? Do the groupings reflect a cohesiveness amongst the class as a whole (Hargreaves, 1967)?

Generally, it appears that the extremely dull child is unlikely to achieve a central position. Intelligence (whatever it is) does seem, as at present measured, to correlate fairly well with popularity, and on the whole friends of *like* intelligence rather than *unlike* intelligence are made. On the other hand, achievement as opposed to intelligence is not necessarily such a good guide. Often, in fact, those of average achievement prove more popular than those of outstanding achievement. Popular children also tend to be better looking and are certainly free from any marked oddities. (From this point of view, it is probably better to be nice-looking and 'dim' than ugly and 'dim', since the former certainly enjoy more social success as a rule!) McCandless, Bilous and Bennett suggest that popular children are better adjusted emotionally. They showed that young children who were popular and socialized well were those that appeared to be less dependent upon adults. Stone and Church (1965) suggest that popular older children are usually fairly self-possessed and 'good-natured'. Those who are seldom chosen tend to have strong interests and hobbies that can be pursued in solitude. They also make the point that popular adolescents depend very much upon social conformity and consensus norms of behaviour (of peers). The marked social deviant is unlikely to be a long-term success.

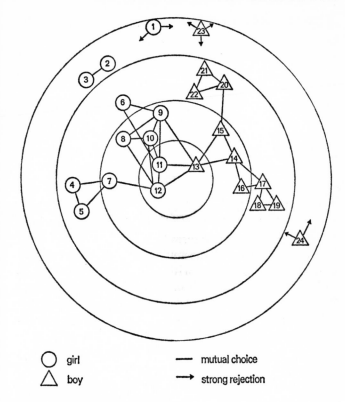

○ girl   —— mutual choice

△ boy   ⟶ strong rejection

Fig. 1. A target sociogram
The sociogram is based on 12 boys and 12 girls
(note loosely linked number of sub-groups amongst
boys)
Children numbered 1-24

3

The teacher's image

To some extent, the image that a teacher has of himself is bound to be influenced by the image society has of him (and it should be remembered that society includes his pupils). The generic term 'teacher' has always led to confusion because of the multiplicity of differently regarded tasks contained within it. Sixty years ago Sir Robert Morant thought it patently ridiculous that there could be any professional organization capable of containing both the Fellow of All Souls College and the reception-class teacher of infants. Be that as it may, there is as yet no totally unified professional organization which caters for the whole gamut of teachers from every institution. Teachers of infants do see themselves as different persons from the teachers of sixth-form children; and the self-image is in part formed from the different cluster of attitudes towards the differing facets of the professional role. These attitudes help to shape the role concepts and certainly affect the role performance.

In a paper read at the Colston Research Society Symposium of 1968 (Taylor, 1969) Ian McMullen said that in the past the sources of the teacher's exposition had been those of his academic background, a possibly limited quantity of reading since and his class textbook; that the teacher had regarded himself as a major source of wisdom and that that source had been mainly verbal. Frequently the teacher was the major source of motivation, mainly through the desire of children to please or not displease him, but also by the intrinsic interest he aroused and the emphasis placed upon examination goals and their utility in future life. He should, too, have been a useful constructor of appropriate situations for the practice of skills and judgement.

The tendency in the past, if one may generalize, has been one of the teacher *not* using the pupils as a rich source of enthusiasm, but of relying upon himself as virtually the only catalyst to action. Not unnaturally, this caricature of the central, all-seeing, autonomous teacher is one that has not only affected the teacher's self-image and his traditional role, but also his personality. Even more important it has meant, as C. M. Fleming has pointed out (1959), that the pupils are very keen both to assess this central, all-pervasive personality and to interact with it on the basis of preconceived expectations. Fleming says, 'The methods employed by pupils in their study of the characteristics of a new teacher are not unlike those standardized in recent years by psychologists engaged on the assessment of temperament, personality or character.' They are summarized as follows:

1. Study of physical characteristics
2. Analysis of expressive movements, voice, gesture, etc.

3. Examination of personal expression through speech, dress, etc.
4. Observation of general conduct (frequency of laughter, anger)
5. Comparison of traits with other human beings found in the same group
6. What Fleming rather euphemistically terms experiments in miniature situations, deliberately devised
7. Tests of persistence, endurance, self-control
8. A study of relevant social background as far as this can be observed.

Teacher as a 'prime source' of knowledge

Few teachers carry out their work without being aware that individuals can modify groups. After all, to some extent they hope to be good examples of just such a process. But this ought to lead us to ask *why* someone takes up teaching in the first place. Is it because of avoidance of the outside world? 'The man amongst boys – the boys amongst men', or 'those who can, do, those who can't teach.' After all, the possibilities for the abuse of power are quite real and sometimes such abuse really does take place. Also the teacher is a communicator, yet isolated to some extent. He remains essentially alone in his classroom. Most teachers feel considerable unease when observed at the task of teaching. Why? Is it because the intimacy of the atmosphere is so sensitive to outside influences? It seems that the teacher likes to feel himself entirely responsible for his own class. (Indeed, I have heard many teachers refer somewhat jealously and possessively to *their* children in a way which not only excluded the other staff from real knowledge of the children, but suggested that the parents knew infinitely less about the child than the teacher!) The success of one's own class or classes is frequently equated with overall success in external examinations or the school play. There are obvious dangers in all this, since if the teacher fails as a 'prime source' for his children he will feel inadequate. If he is faced with questions he cannot answer *too frequently*, the children may well treat him with contempt. To attempt to hold the position of 'professional knowall' is untenable in the long run and may well earn the contempt of adults as well as children. McMullen feels that teacher insecurity can lead to much opposition to new curricula, since over the years a teacher builds up knowledge of the subject he is teaching and the pitfalls to be avoided in teaching it. A new curriculum will involve either much work in mastering the new material (followed by the consequent period of insecurity in using it) or the admission to the children that he is learning it too. Some teachers find the latter situation intolerable. Quite possibly it is fear that causes the teacher to resist methods of organization which might upset the delicate balance of the position which he has set up for himself in the group.

Characteristics of teachers

P. E. Vernon (1953) maintains that, 'Teachers are as diverse in their psychological traits as any other occupational group', and that, 'it is fallacious to talk of the teaching personality as something distinct and consistent.' This view is not the only one, however. There are others who feel that there are some measurable similarities in the traits and attitudes of all teachers – at least enough to establish some sort of stereotype. During this decade interest in the teacher has been growing. More work is being undertaken into the teacher's self-concepts, the role of the teacher (Westwood, 1967), the language of the teacher and its efficacy (Barnes, 1969). A good deal of work has likewise been done on the attitudes of student-teachers, personality and work potential. Cattell has shown that U.S. teachers rank high on such traits as warm-heartedness; and Lamke reported that factors such as warm-heartedness and spontaneity were of some significance in distinguishing between good and bad teachers. Extant English research does not come to such marked conclusions.

To return to Vernon's summary of 1953, he says that probably most of those in teaching who are well adjusted are 'somewhat extroverted, but that (probably) many other personality types do excellent work and [that] there are certainly large numbers of misfits. Extremely various also are the ideals, sentiments and interest, and psychological mechanisms underlying the choice of and continuance in the profession' (Vernon, 1953). In a book called *The Adolescent Personality*, Blos (1941) suggested that, 'in the life of every adult the phase of adolescence has left unresolved conflicts in its wake, and final emotional stabilization has been achieved by compromise and other devices.' He thinks that this may account for the sensitivity with which a teacher handles one situation and the clumsiness with which he handles another. The teacher feels closer to those pupils whose problems are more akin to his own. The teacher may be unaware of this, but Blos avers that the teacher needs to understand not only the mechanisms of the pupils' minds and personalities – but also his own. He points out that self-awareness is an essential concomitant for all those choosing to work with children. Whatever the case may be, there is certainly enough evidence to suggest that the personality of the teacher does critically affect the performance of the pupils (Vernon) and certainly every teacher drags into the classroom the residues of his own childhood (Morris, 1967).

D. G. Ryans directed large-scale research into the characteristics of teachers (Ryans, 1961); and, using factorial analysis upon the massive amount of material collected, he identified 'three major clusters of observable teacher-behaviour'. These clusters can be best thought of as dimensions or continua, e.g. pattern X constituted warm, friendly behaviour versus aloof, egocentric, restricted teacher behaviour; pattern Y constituted the responsible, systematic behaviour versus unplanned, slipshod and evasive behaviour; and pattern Z consisted of imaginative and enthusiastic behaviour versus dull and routine teacher behaviour. Ryans found that those teachers who rated positively in such dimensions were most likely to:

1. Appraise generously the motives and behaviour of others
2. Be interested in literature and the arts in general
3. Enjoy social groups including relationships with pupils
4. Prefer permissive classroom behaviour.

Ryans also found that pupil behaviour was more re-

active in the elementary school than in the secondary
school (i.e. the teacher impinged more upon the pupils).
He surmised that this was probably because the older
student's behaviour tended towards more independence
and was 'self-generated' whereas the younger child was
more likely to look to the teacher for cues to his own
behaviour. There is also some evidence to show that
teachers' personality characteristics can have different
effects on different kinds of pupils (Washburne and
Heil, 1960); and also a book by Bush (1954) which calls
into question the notion of affectivity and involvement.
Bush suggested that too much warmth was dangerous
and militated against objectivity.

Motives for teaching and personal qualities

Earlier I briefly touched upon the question of motive.
Why do we teach? Why aren't we bank-clerks, stock-
brokers, or architects? Some sociologists suggest that
teaching is a good career choice if one requires a ladder
for upward social mobility (always assuming a relatively low level of socio-economic status in the beginning!). Others might suggest a love of children or
an intense wish to go on studying some particular
academic subject; and still others, the need for directing
the psyche to outward situations and the need for power
over others. Whatever the reasons may be, Wiseman
(1965) maintains that the teacher's motive and his self-
image are constantly reflected throughout the teaching
process. He says, 'Those of us who cling to the image
of the teacher as a didactic figure engaged in the skilful
and patient unfolding of a logical sequence of facts and
ideas would be better advised to abandon this concept.'

He goes on to say that the teacher should be seen as a 'controller and manipulator' of the intellectual environment. He also makes the point that much teacher training is so woefully weak that the teachers thus trained emerge unable to enthuse or manipulate the environment in a way beneficial to the children.

A slightly different point of view is put foward by G. H. Bantock (1967). He makes it clear that, in his opinion, the so-called 'progressive' teachers often shy away from the notion of teacher personality, in the sense not of denying one, but of preferring to think that the teacher should not have an impact upon the learner. Such 'progressives' appear to believe in the role of 'inter-mediator', pointing to the elements of importance in the classroom situation and then allowing the situation to do the work. This may be all very well; it is indeed often quite appropriate to particular learning situations. But the teachers who managed to inspire me were not thus disengaged. *They* were Bantock's 'spell-binders', Wiseman's 'manipulators', whose personalities were dynamic enough to make an impact upon me. The quietly efficient disengaged I have forgotten; the slightly mad, mathematical musician stays with me, and with me his enthusiasms, long after he is dead. Again, as Bantock says,

> However free the situation may seem to be within which the child is to learn, the very intensity with which he follows his own self-activity within the experimental framework will in part depend upon the implicit or explicit expectations he infers from his teachers.

However, too dominating or power-seeking a person tends to activate a vicious circle of troublesome and further repression. As early as 1945 Anderson and Brewer of the University of Illinois, studying 'dominative' and 'integrative' features of teachers' personalities, found that this was the case (Anderson, 1945).

In England, summaries on the personal qualities of teachers have been fairly well represented, more particularly by one person, K. M. Evans, and, as she says, most of the work on the personality of the teacher has been pretty inconclusive. Some of the tests used in these studies have been applicable to anyone (such as the Allport–Vernon–Lindzey Study of Values and the Bernreuter Personality Inventory). In addition, some tests have been especially designed for teachers and there are a number of attitude scales concerned with the qualities exhibited by the teacher in the classroom. There is, too, the well-known Minnesota Teacher Attitude Inventory, though this latter has not been used much in England until relatively recently. (In 1963 Herbert and Turnbull published a study of students in training which suggested that the M.T.A.I. did distinguish between the more and less successful students.) On the whole K. M. Evans thinks it unlikely that the M.T.A.I. would be a satisfactory instrument for use in the selection of students for teaching. She says, 'Even though differences between mean scores of more and less successful students may be significant, the high standard deviations generally reported point to a considerable overlapping of scores in the two groups and consequent difficulty of discrimination among individual members' (Evans, 1967).

If one were to 'cull' a stereotype from a mixture of both popular child-folklore and research here and in the States, it seems that for England the stereotype personality of the teacher might well seem to be 'conservative, conformist and dull', whilst for the States that of 'domineering, ultra-conventional and self-centred': a depressing picture. But is it true? If so what causes it? In a book called *The American College* edited by Sanford, there is an article by G. G. Stern (1962) in which he writes, 'The vast majority of institutions examined thus far are characterized by environments that emphasize some degree of conformity and constraint.' The inference is that conformity and constraint become ingrained in the students. Also, since the teacher must often act as the high priest of tradition, he must perforce appear traditionalist and conservative. Another aspect which is interesting is that there is evidence that teaching tends to attract a fairly large proportion of the slightly less academic. Jersild (1955) says that it is possible for a teacher to think that he is motivated by a desire to advance knowledge when in fact it is actually a means of expressing competitive drives in order to gain recognition and to overcome the feeling that he is not much good. Certainly, all teachers ought perhaps to be aware of this since, as Jersild says, 'The teacher's understanding and acceptance of himself is the most important requirement in any effort he makes to help students to know themselves and to gain healthy attitudes of self-acceptance.'

4

Teacher interaction styles

Communication structure

The interaction of the teacher and the children is one of the most important aspects of the educative process and possibly one of the more neglected. To some extent the type and quality of the interaction will determine not only the effectiveness of the learning situation but the attitudes, interests and in part even the personality of the pupils. Classroom organization is not merely the ordering of people and materials, it is one of the vital aspects of the teacher–pupil relationship which depends upon a mixture of forethought, planning, a good communication structure and, to some extent, discipline. The traditional type of classroom communication is still to be seen in many schools and is obviously important. This is the process of teacher-to-children instructions and the process of co-action, i.e. relationship between teacher and separate pupils. Often effective, often extremely inefficient, it means the patient (or impatient) 'queuing' by children all waiting their turn for advice, reward, or reinforcement in some form. (In a talk to the staff of the University of Bristol School of Education in spring 1969, Professor Philip Jackson of

Chicago referred to the traditions of time-wasting in schools in both the States and England. Teacher waiting 'to see if Liza had a listening face' he called it, and 'queuing for consultation'.)

Another type of relationship is beginning to be more and more exploited in learning situations, that of real interaction and of full communication flow. In this relationship the structure of the group is one where communication takes place among all members of the group (including the teacher) with equal facility.

The power to decide what type of classroom structure should prevail does not solely rest with the teacher, since he is by no means a free agent in this matter. Indeed, as in most matters concerned with education, tradition looms large in the background. At secondary-school level a mixture of both tradition and concrete survival tactics usually demands that the teacher 'defines' the situation before the pupils do.

'With the C and D streams, as we shall see, this attempt by the pupils to undermine the teacher's definition may persist over long periods. As one Lumley teacher reported: "Either you murder them, or they'll murder you. Either you win or they win. And I'll tell you, mate, I'm the one that's going to win"' (Hargreaves, 1967).

The implication here is that certain groups of children may present collective attitudes hostile to anything other than the teacher behaving in the way which they expect him to behave. Thus, a fully interactive style of teaching is more permissible (and feasible) at certain early levels of education, is very dependent upon type of school, headteacher and subject, and is catered for at advanced levels in different ways, with a real hiatus

33

occurring somewhere between ten and sixteen years. That is to say that the type of school, the age level, the type of child, the subject taught (and to some extent the community context), all contribute to an atmosphere encouraging the permitting or enforcing of one or other form of classroom control. Interaction in a modern English state primary school now seems entirely appropriate at almost any time, but interaction in an English or French university lecture is relatively rare and is usually deemed inappropriate. With university expansion, larger seminars and the demise of the tutorial system, when does every student get the chance to do more than listen to his tutors?

When talking of teacher styles and classroom communication, it is impossible to describe the one perfect or most effective type of teacher–child or teacher–student relationship. Styles will necessarily depend upon a host of variables, and classroom verbal behaviour is not the sole indication of style, though it is a very important one (Barnes, 1969). 'Studying the activities of teachers in the classroom without at the same time analysing the actions of students would give a distorted and incomplete view of the teaching process' (Bellack *et al.*, 1966).

Categories of teaching style

Observation of student-teachers on teaching practice has led me to categorize roughly three nodal points along the continuum of teaching style. The intermediate stages seem very difficult to discern without knowing a great deal about both the teacher and taught. But these three points or styles did seem fairly recognizable.

1. The teacher who retains all control and is entirely dominant – a teacher-centred style. (There is sometimes little contact with children.)
2. The teacher who allows the children actively to participate in the decision-making as part of the organization and management of learning – a child-centred style perhaps.
3. The teacher who has absolutely no impact upon the group, whose organization fails and who is not able to provide any structure for learning. (There is often no contact with children.)

One and three might almost be represented as Scylla and Charybdis, with safe steerage being infinitely more difficult than in legends of old.

From the point of view of satisfaction, the second seems to be more beneficial to the children as a whole (though even here there can be dangers, particularly with young or very young children needing optimum security). As regards efficiency of learning (measured in terms of subject matter attainment), taking one and two, neither seems consistently superior. From the point of view of motivation over lengthy periods and of furthering 'divergent' thinking, a child-centred approach does seem somewhat superior, though this is in itself open to all sorts of interpretations. Recent though rather hysterical reactions in England against child-centred approaches do not nullify the more serious criticisms of certain aspects of 'progressive' education. Certainly, for primary education, Dearden, in a recent book (1968) makes one aware of the dangers of excessive claims for democracy in the classroom and of the uncritical application of 'free' approaches with concomitant haphazard learning.

Motivation of learners does seem to be one of the key factors in teacher–pupil relationships. It is certainly a common source from which the power of the teacher is derived. The structure of the group can rarely be such that it ignores the teacher, unless of course the teacher is entirely ineffectual. The teacher has much that is still vested in his role by the value system of the prevailing culture that also lends him power. Children are forced to attend school. The teacher may also force them or reward them. He may so enthuse and involve the child that the child identifies with him (referent power), or so impress the child with his expertise that the child actively seeks guidance.

In practice there is usually a subtle blend of all these; anyway, it should be remembered that although the style of interaction can be predominantly 'set' by the teacher, it does not depend solely upon him. Different pupils will respond differently to different kinds of teachers.

Classroom climate: learning and control

Mark Twain's image of two people sitting on a log, teacher at one end and pupil at the other, does not tell us enough about the layers of the relationship; e.g. the obvious, on-the-surface, *manifest layer* of relationship may be immediately apparent. But the *intentional layer*, where feelings, motives and intent are considered, is not so immediately discernible.

Kerkman and Wright (1961) used photographic analysis as one of their main tools in investigating the pupil–teacher structure and found that 'co-active' teaching produced two usual types of pupil–teacher response:

1. 'Attending to the teacher possibly with supplicant hand upraised'
2. 'Actually engaging the teacher' (shouts of 'Sir' or 'Miss').

As Philip Jackson said, the first is grossly inefficient and slows down the whole learning process, while the second is plainly disruptive and a nuisance to all concerned. Kerkman and Wright suggested that consistent use of one pattern was probably much less desirable than a variation of patterns, since individual circumstances altered so much according to the learning context. Furthermore, they corroborate my earlier comment by saying, 'The use of the small group with a more open form of communication is likely to produce greater involvement of the learner and it is likely in the long run to produce independent and responsible student action.' Naturally the optimum balance of structural pattern is largely a matter of conjecture unless the specific circumstances are known. Also, Kerkman and Wright found *age* of children to be a significant factor in all this. The older children were more able to involve themselves independently and organize themselves. Also, more informal 'interactive' situations seem likely to occur in schools in the smaller communities and where the schools themselves are small. (This is certainly true within my experience as regards urban and country primary schools in England.)

But an understanding of the classroom climate not only illuminates the teacher's position in relation to learning, it also illuminates the matter of control. Withall (1951) developed an index system for assessing the quality of the teacher's control. The trouble is that, like the work of Bellack and others, it depended upon the language of the teacher for its seven categories. Nevertheless, it does afford an opportunity for systematic classification and charting of teacher behaviour, and simply an awareness of the categories and of the reason for their adoption by Withall is a salutary experience. Let me quote part of category six:

Reproving, disapproving or disparaging statements or questions

By means of these statements a teacher may express complete or partial disapproval of the ideas, behaviour and, to him, personality weaknesses of the learner. The teacher's internalized societal values largely enter into these responses. By means of these statements some teachers believe they are fulfilling their responsibility of inculcating in young people society's standards of acceptable and desirable behaviour and achievement.

Various others (Lewin as early as 1939) have tried to label the different styles of teaching in different ways, i.e. as directive or non-directive, child-centred or teacher-centred, authoritarian or democratic. However classified, it would probably be true to say that nowadays, both among children and adults, there is a climate of opinion that is opposed to the indiscriminate use of coercive power in general and that this climate of opinion is begining to be noticeable in the classroom. Such a situation also serves to underline the ambivalent role of the teacher in the modern society's knowledge explosion (Jenkins, 1966).

5

The teacher's place in society

Historical and cultural determinants

For a tribe to survive as an integral unit it must have some way of handing on its customs and its language. The children need to learn the language and the elementary rules of behaviour, feeding habits and their position in the family. Eventually, these same children must be trained in the crafts necessary for their livelihood. Often, at adolescence, the children have to be admitted to the rites and customs by which adult members live. Very often, in primitive communities, mothers and other women teach the children what and how to eat and speak. Fathers and other men teach the children how to hunt, fish or grow crops (though here the sex difference must be borne in mind); and the medicine men or witch-doctors initiate the young into much of the tribal lore and culture. Hoyle says, 'Primitive societies do not as a rule have "teachers" in the sense of persons whose specialized role in society is to instruct the young. The child acquires a knowledge of his culture through the process of socialization, and in

39

these societies socialization is synonymous with education' (Hoyle, 1969). He says that, with some exceptions
(such as the Poro schools of West Africa), the distinctive role of teacher does not appear until the emergence
of the so-called intermediate societies of India, Greece,
Rome, etc., and that in such societies the role is concomitant with the transfer of the culture of the elite
to their children.

In the past women traditionally taught the infants
and girls of the tribe and, as a very general rule, no
man would condescend to teach infants to speak or girls
to cook, whereas the initiation rites and rituals were
often entrusted to the special guardians of the culture
(the priests) and these guardians enjoyed a very privi-
leged status. (I see a slight connection between them
and the present-day university teachers who often
appear to see themselves as preservers of past tradition
rather than agents of cultural renewal!) However that
may be, one should bear in mind that there was little
normal possibility of promotion from, say, mother-
nurse to master craftsman to priest witch-doctor. The
three functions were not thought of as being at all similar, as far as one can make out. In fact, it is a very
modern idea to think of all functions as being part and
parcel of the same profession. Also, in Europe, from the
start the writing masters and the teachers of the poor
had a status considerably inferior to that of the school-
master-cleric who taught the 'high culture' of the 'tribe'
to the sons of the elite. With the rise of mass institutionalized education such dividing lines became blurred
and, with much internecine strife, the large amorphous
body of the teaching profession gradually emerged.
This is of course a highly simplistic view of what is

really a complicated set of historical and cultural determinants of the role of the teacher. What of other
determinants more applicable today?

First, teaching is still regarded by many as a voca-
tion, with all that this implies, including very often the
demanding of superior or different moral and spiritual
qualities to those exhibited in the general cultural context or the community. Second, dismissal for actual
incompetent teaching seems fairly rare (dismissal for
common assault or moral turpitude is somewhat more
likely); third, community pressures are very strong. The
acceptance of these pressures must have its effect upon
those who teach and those who think of teaching. Conformity seems almost a prerequisite.

In England it is still possible to trace the different
determinants of the three main bodies of teachers
though the groups themselves are rather compressed
and divisions blurred. The witch-doctors of our culture
(university teachers) are still fairly highly respected if
not well rewarded. They are still thought of as being
men of deep wisdom and not inconsiderable scholar-
ship. They enjoy more self-government than do most
teachers, often work in attractive and prestigious sur-
roundings and have the chance of travel and additional
earnings as part of their job. (Many will no doubt be sur-
prised at the omission on my part of long holidays as a
significant feature in the life of university staff. My experience leads me to believe that these are more
imagined than real, since many university teachers use
the long 'vacations' for essential research work and for
adding to their knowledge.) Secondary teachers do not
in general enjoy the same regard or opportunities enjoyed by university teachers. There is also some evi-

dence to suggest that they *may* enter secondary teaching, particularly those who are graduates, only after they have failed to gain entry to the profession of their choice or because the class of their degree was disappointingly low. There is also some evidence (Floud and Scott, 1961) that they come from the same classes as clergymen, journalists and bank-clerks, from what one might term the typically middle or lower middle classes. Frequently, if such teachers come from a college of education they will have already experienced rejection in the form of having been denied entrance to a university in the first place. Indeed, there is some danger that a certain percentage of young men and women entrants to the profession are a disappointed group and possibly some are of a somewhat lower calibre than those who join the other professions. There is always the danger, too, that many certificated teachers (and this is still the majority in this country), may feel that their higher education and training was sadly lacking. Some feel that the college of education is to the university what the secondary modern school was to the grammar school, i.e. lacking in prestige and quality and not rigorous in the application of its principles. This is not to deny, however, that some colleges of education are more truly educative and liberal than many a university college. They also have the merit of containing some of the only teachers in higher education who have at least been trained to teach and moreover who are appointed quite often because they can teach.

What of the elementary teacher? Historically, elementary teaching has often been the only avenue open to the working class if more than a cursory education was desired. In addition, 'Public elementary education has its roots firmly set in the charitable institutions set up as relief measures by the rich.... The first elementary teachers were women, cripples or men unable to do hard physical work' (King-Hall *et al.*, 1953). By and large the teacher in the pre-industrial society was involved in teaching values, values which helped to preserve the structure of society as it was then conceived, whereas in a complex industrial society the preparation of children for future occupational roles (and possibly the frequent change of these roles) becomes more and more important. Institutionalized education tends to become increasingly utilitarian as such a society develops; and closer and closer links are made between centres of learning and industry, hospitals, factories, commerce and the arts (Kerr, 1963). Even at the primary level there have been significant movements by the schools and teachers towards serving the community. In many urban areas the primary schools are open from early in the morning till late at night as playgrounds where there is supervision and relative safety. Play-groups and clubs, meals supervision and sports facilities are all provided by the schools and often by dedicated and over-worked teachers.

Popular myth has it, however, that those drawn into teaching smaller children are those dedicated to spinsterhood, i.e. fulfilling the mother-nurse category as best they can. Untrue though this may be, it presents a popular stereotype that even the large losses of young women teachers to motherhood cannot dispel.

The teaching task

In general, all three groups of teachers have similar elements in their tasks however different the specifics may be. In the present century these elements seem to be:

1. To present some part (there are arguments as to which part) of the accumulated knowledge of the past and transmit it to the pupil of today with some reference to the present
2. To cater for the dynamics of change by taking his present knowledge and relating it as far as possible to the world in which his pupils will be adults (i.e. at very least the teacher of, say, young adolescents must understand some of the major trends in contemporary civilization and prepare the young adequately for the problems they will encounter as they approach maturity).

Many, of course, hold that this second is not enough. They would urge that the teacher should be an active agent for change and reform. There are, too, official policies which shape the functions in a positive way. (The Plowden Report on Children and their Primary Schools is just such a one.) The teacher is encouraged to reinforce certain trends and oppose others. There is also the crucial ambiguity reflected in these two main elements of the teacher's role. They can often be mutually exclusive!

Ottaway, in *Education and Society* (1962), points out that one of the prime tasks of any teacher is that of handing on 'the cultural values and behaviour patterns of the society to its young and potential members', and

44

I have said that, paradoxically, in addition to reflecting a given social system, an equally important task for education is that of providing 'critical and creative individuals able to make new inventions and discoveries and willing to initiate change'. Every teacher, in whichever function and at whatever level, therefore takes part in preserving the established order whilst at the same time providing for the dynamics of change. There is thus inherent conflict in much that is conceived of as the teacher's role if that teacher is expected to prepare individuals for new and better forms of society whilst ensuring that the societal and cultural norms are not too quickly jettisoned.

Put differently, in any complex industrial-technical society, teachers become a social necessity, since the diffusion of basic skills, such as literacy, and the provision of technocrats are of prime importance for the nation's survival. At the same time, in such a society, the teacher is increasingly expected to stimulate the child to accept certain social values (particularly if large numbers of 'followers' are necessary for political systems, economic production, or the exploitation of certain raw materials). With any reduction of the family contribution in socialization, and particularly if both parents are working, the role of the teacher becomes more of a multiple role adding further functions to an already diffuse role complex. The teacher therefore rapidly arrives at the point whereby he must presumably:

1. Fulfil the multiple objectives of the modern state educational system
2. Be a member of a particular institution and relate

45

    to hierarchical role positions within an organizational framework
3. Relate to parents and pupils within a particular community context and need
4. Fulfil his obligations as an adherent of his own social grouping and profession.

All this means that the schoolteacher (rather more than the university teacher) has to perform tasks which are not only concerned with imparting a body of knowledge, but also with the inculcation of attitudes, the development of habits and skills, the strengthening of loyalties and the reinforcement of moral codes. Wilson (1962) maintains that the effect of the dynamics of operating these tasks upon *status* is very marked and suggests that the teacher has been forced to spread his talents very thinly. He goes on to say that he is not judged by his remarkable versatility, but rather by his lack of depth in the separate areas in which he works. I think that, in varying degrees, this is probably true at almost all levels of teaching, since more and more peripheral roles gravitate towards institutions of learning as education, training and retraining become more necessary in a technological society.

Selecting and socializing

'In a complex industrial society with a wide diversity of social roles, where basic education is obligatory for everyone, social selection – the allocation of individuals to particular occupations within society – occurs within the educational system rather than, as in the case of traditional societies, before education is embarked upon' (Wilson). This is a very important point, since it relates to much that is central to the work of any teacher; i.e. the distribution of what Jean Floud terms 'life chances' (Floud, 1962). Such distribution becomes an important part of the institutional machinery. Record cards, reading ages, suitability profiles, intelligence tests, attainment tests, language ability and style, class positions, reports, external examinations, college and university records: all these and much more constitute merely a part of the mechanism of grading, assessing, reinforcing and allocating. It is a process which many pupils and ex-pupils view with extreme distrust and contempt. Thus, if the child or young adult is to be prepared for some social role other than that of its father and mother, it is largely the teacher who becomes responsible for that preparation. The process of selection becomes a major concern of the teacher. There is a tendency for many to believe that this process of selection only becomes crucial towards the end of the period of full-time education. In a society such as ours, where over half the state primary schools 'stream' or 'ability group' their pupils in various ways, such a belief seems inappropriate, to say the least. Further, it must be remembered that much of this process of stratification and selection is started by the age of seven or earlier.

As more and more women go out to work, there is a tendency to 'offload' many of the former family socializing tasks onto the teacher. 'The teacher,' says Wilson, 'has taken over from the parent some of the activities of socializing the child,' and has in fact become the 'social weaning' agent for our industrial society. At the same time as a considerable part of the

47

socializing task has passed to the teacher, the task of inducing motivation has become more and more critical, particularly if the society only pays 'lip-service' to the values which it still insists teachers should be representing to the pupils. There is, too, the element of 'middle-class' value transmission which, it has been suggested, is a strong factor in the English school system. Certainly, there is very often a transmission and reinforcement of values appropriate to the stratum in which the brighter child will move, and much of this can be related to the social class of teachers, their training and their language styles. However, one of the advantages of the movement towards less rigid ability-grouping systems in schools is that, as Forum says, 'The abolition of streaming, therefore, implies the restoration to the teacher of his creative role as an educator' (Simon, 1964).

The erosion of the coercive props of authority, the introduction of more flexible organization and the lessening in streaming and grading require that the teacher should have a basic sympathy with the child which is not dissimilar to that of the parent. Increasingly, the teacher is in no position to compel fearful learning on pain of retribution and this process is not accomplished without strain. Parents, teachers and children often have different expectations and emphasize different aspects of the educative process (Musgrove and Taylor, 1969). But the increased mobility of today's society is tending to reconcile the parents to the teacher's influence on the child. At the same time there is a tendency for English teachers and parents to begin to move closer together than has been the case in the past; since, if the teacher is to be a meaningful socializer and sometimes to remedy the omissions of the home he must be in a position to foster a sustained relationship with the child. Such a relationship cannot be provided automatically by legislation or institution, though I feel that better training for administrative roles and the provision of a school counselling service would greatly facilitate it.

Diffuseness and affectivity

Some writers have tried to specify the various sub-roles of the teacher in considerable detail (Ridl and Wattenberg, 1951). Others like Blyth (1965) and Wilson (1962) have talked more in terms of socialization, diffuseness and affectivity. An exhaustive list of sub-roles applicable to all seems in any case an impossibility (or certainly so at this time when there has been relatively little research as yet). The notions of diffuseness and affectivity are important, however, for they enable us to categorize some of the main types of teaching as well as telling us something about the teacher's position outside the classroom and in it.

Because the teacher's role behaviour is so much affected by his personality, because his tasks are so many and varied and because the business of socializing, inspiring and encouraging children is so difficult to 'determine', the teacher's role can be termed diffuse. The very diffuseness of the teacher's task means that to society in general it may seem non-expert, less urgent and not very dramatic. Also, the very fact that all people have had some experience of education (sometimes not very enjoyable!) tends to bestow on them an attitude of 'willingness to advise or criticize' which can be very galling to a teacher. There is, too, the fact that because teaching is a normal large-scale need of our society, it necessitates a very much larger task force (often not very selectively chosen or trained) than many other professions, and this has had its effect upon social status and reward. In fact, the expansion of education for all means that whether teachers have high abilities or not they have to be accepted because large numbers are needed. Thus, colleges of education do not fail many students and graduates merely by being graduates are still thought equipped to teach. Of course, figures of failures at end of college courses are not a true indication of the failure rate, as many colleges weed out unlikely teachers during the course. Also, from 1972 onwards all graduates entering *school* teaching will have to be trained. There are signs, too, that the universities are beginning to consider the in-service training of their new lecturers, though no doubt many academics will continue to practise in universities despite their total ineptitude for teaching, and to suggest that there is a real movement in this country towards the training of university teachers would certainly be to misrepresent facts.

The teacher, and particularly the teacher of young children, is often so totally involved that warmth of personality and affective concern for his charges are implicit in his role, and *affectivity* becomes vital to the teaching process. This has its dangers – not only because of the possibilities of over-concern and an emotional involvement which might cloud the teacher's judgement and lessen objectivity – but for the image which it has cast outward into society; the image of the essentially motherly *female* teacher. In a society which has not yet truly achieved the emancipation of women as regards jobs, social esteem and salary, this surely militates against the image of professional expertise and seriousness to some extent. The affective teacher of young children may appear to be merely fulfilling the functions of mother substitute, of child-minding. 'She loves small children,' one might hear said, 'so we thought she would be a good infant teacher' (Evans, 1967). Everyone who loves small children is not necessarily going to be a worthwhile educator of them, or at least that is my experience in a college of education. But still the myth is perpetuated. Nevertheless, affectivity is important, vital at the lower-age range and very often varying in degree according to the age of the pupils. The notion does help us to classify some of the differing aspects of the teacher's task, providing we remember its relationship to the personality of the teacher as well as to that of the pupil.

6

Aspects of personality, self and others in the classroom

Personality and notions of 'wholeness'

The study of personality is probably one of the most interesting studies in which man has ever engaged. Man, in fact, is so fascinating and rewarding a study in himself that there has been no lack of interested students – or of theories. But though the study of personality is central to much of the work in the behavioural sciences, psychologists are not by any means in complete agreement over what it is or exactly how it relates to genetic background and socialization experience. However, as Peel (1956) says, all the definitions seem to stress 'the point of uniqueness, organization and wholeness', and there is usually some coherent and cohesive pattern in a person's reactions to his environment which are thought to reflect his personality. A confusing plethora of ideas and beliefs, explanations and opinions exist, so that at first sight it might appear almost impossible for the teacher of children to steer a safe educationists' course between neuro-psychology, social psychology, ego-psychology, social philosophy and so on. Yet the fact that personality theory has drawn upon many basic areas, that some psychologists (such as Sherif and Cantril) suggest that we are *persons* only when we have met society and developed attitudes, whereas others (such as Allport) suggest we are persons first and then members of society, is on the whole of little concern to the teacher. Whilst acknowledging and recognizing the debt that education owes to Freud and Erikson, Skinner and Hull, neither their relative merits and demerits, nor even the occasional circularity of the argument need concern the beginning teacher. As teachers we should be more concerned with the notions of 'wholeness' stressed by Peel, more interested in the *growth* towards maturity and the fostering of a development that enriches and furthers whatever may already be latent in the pupil (though entering the caveat that such potential should in no wise be developed at the expense of the potential of others).

If a child is to achieve a fully rounded and integrated personality as an adult, he must receive consistent, meaningful recognition of his worth and talent. This will not mean the mere recognition of his intelligence and attainment, but the appreciation and understanding of his emotions, temperament, interests and attitudes as well; and this is almost as formidable a task *with* psychology as without it, for no teacher is well placed for constant and exclusive attention to one child.

In general, though it may be true that different conduct, attitudes and values are expected of the individual as he grows, teachers cannot be too careful in their hesitancy over the mere rewarding of conformity. At all times, the individual must be encouraged to believe in himself, his own worth, his possibilities and in the reciprocal nature of his relationships with others. For the teacher it is sometimes easier to think in terms of the general good of the class, group or school and extremely difficult indeed to equate such with the general good of each individual. This becomes especially difficult if the teacher himself has a personality unsuited to the task, or in which the residues of childhood have stunted or diminished a maturity effective and affective in its concern for others.

The self-image and significant others

Physiological factors and social expectations

Physiological factors, such as size, muscular development and looks do seem to play a part in so much as they affect other people's attitudes and expectations. Such expectations can effect a 'feedback' to the person concerned in such a way as to destroy, confirm or exaggerate that person's existing self-concept. It is worthwhile remembering how many people associate round, fat people with jovial, comfort-loving sociable types, and thin people with restraint, tension, introversion, excessive ambition etc. Indeed, in the past temperaments used to be associated with bodily types. Once stereotypes or 'traditions' of this sort have been built up, they themselves can have a radical effect upon some of the moulding influences and norms operating in the socialization process. Certainly, personality can be associated with chemical balance, particularly with the action of the pituitary, thyroid, gonads and adrenals. In addition, various external factors can affect the personality, such as the use of drugs, a lack of food, diet, disease and sexual behaviour.

Social factors are often closely related to the physiological ones, since the individual cannot normally be viewed out of the context of his social environment and learns to play roles and acquire codes of conduct which become internalized. Introjection processes seem most crucial during early childhood, but one should not forget the power of the teacher here since he must often act both as preceptor, model and planner. He must allow for and tolerate fashions and fads and the rapid assimilation of new roles (particularly if he is teaching adolescents), and in part facilitate situations in which role change can be feasible and safe.

All social groups tend to seek to enforce certain rules upon members. As the child grows older it is usually the peer group which acts as a major factor affecting the personality of the child. Nuances of behaviour, accents, attitudes and fashions all play their part, a not always desirable part in the eyes of many parents and teachers. Of course, from a very early age, one comes to play a variety of roles and however rigid a group it is it usually permits some latitude in this. The non-resolution of conflicting role-expectations can be particularly devastating to the healthy development of the personality. Friends', parents' and teachers' expectations are not necessarily synonymous. Often, to an adolescent looking for reflections which will help to confirm his identity, conflicting expectations can be near-disastrous. Indeed, in order to evaluate themselves most adolescents seem to need to experiment with the feelings and behaviour of self and others. They are concerned with how they are viewed by others and need recognition and confirmation as well as the chance to contribute if they are to achieve an identity of their own. (Erik Erikson maintains that the study of identity has become as important to our time as the study of sexuality was to Freud's. He points out that, during adolescence, a youth rarely identifies with his parents.)

Personality, motivation and learning

In the context of personality as it affects learning, the child's reactions to success, failure, praise and blame become crucial – crucial since they relate not only to the pupil's social and emotional behaviour in the class-room, but also to motivation. Most people know the formula 'motivation plus ability equals success', in short that many other factors besides ability combine to affect the degree of success or failure to learn. In particular, the attitudes of the children to the teacher are very important. Motivation can also be enhanced or damaged by the attitude of the teacher to the pupil. Dottrens (1962) suggests that the motivation of the child has a great effect upon the teacher as well as the pupil; and says that it 'has on the one hand an internal aspect in which growth, physiological states and acquired experience all play a part, and, on the other hand, an external aspect involving the over-all situation and a specific stimulus'. Most children are aware of the external aspect, since 'if the aims are fixed or the stimulus provided' (by someone with sufficient prestige in the eyes of the child – grown-ups, parents, teachers), 'the pupil will generally make an effort to reach the aims in question, unless they appear to him to be manifestly unattainable.' The motivation of the school child is then often that of a person under considerable pressure. The incentives may be almost entirely of a negative kind and the child's drive towards certain goals in direct conflict with the teaching task; e.g. J. K., a small boy in one class I had, said, 'My Dad says he can't read and he earns a hundred pounds a week, so why the hell should I bother!'

Few adults cannot remember instances when the failure to learn or to enjoy the learning has been more from fear or dislike of the teacher than from dislike of the subject matter to be learned. Many of our basic motives are fundamental or innate drives which are present from birth (e.g. hunger, escape motives, curiosity), and, on the whole our motivation seems to lean towards security, pleasure and the opportunity for some achievement. The wise teacher may well be able to exploit these whenever the opportunity arises. But probably more important are those motives which are acquired, such as attitudes, interests and a sense of purpose. These can represent both the raw materials and the tools of the trade to the teacher and need handling with extreme care if the development rather than the stultification of the individual is to be the end result. It must be remembered that at any time learning in schools is affected by a mixture of both the innate and the acquired drives, and that for any one person a particular motive or drive may be dominant. Further, what has been said about the personality in general and the motives and attitudes in the classroom apply to both the teacher and the child and will vary considerably from individual to individual.

The peer group, the teacher and the child's self-concept

Apart from the family, which is the principal agency for socialization, let us consider who are the really significant others in the pupil's life. Probably first in order of precedence must come the peer group. This operates both within and without the school system. It is usually made up of children of about the same age whose members will have different statuses within the group. Although it may often have customs and a definite organization, the peer group is not thought of as being an established *institutional* factor in its influence upon a person. Elkin (1960) says, 'The child as he develops and moves in changing circles, ordinarily participates in a succession of peer groups', that he may belong to several at the same time and, 'for each group to which he belongs, he has the status of group member – with its accompanying expectations of thought and behaviour. As a new member of an ongoing group, a child is socialized into its patterns; as an established member he helps socialize others and evolve new patterns.'

Second in order of precedence comes the teacher. He is part of a recognized institution which represents the adult society and certain consensus norms of culture and tradition to the child. Over the family he has certain advantages and disadvantages. Advantages in the sense that the child has to attend his school and in that there are established rules and an organizational framework, which facilitate the implanting of certain patterns of behaviour, roles, hierarchy and traditions. Disadvantages in that the teacher can rarely be concerned with the 'whole' child (unless it is a boarding school), in

that many of the school *mores* may not be well sup-
ported outside the school, both in the local community
and society in general, and in that many of the 'props'
to the teacher's authority are more imagined than real.
Further, the teacher's authority having been eroded to
some extent, means that he has to be much more of an
opinion leader and manipulator if he is to win approval,
involve children, and further the ends of learning. As
stated in the previous chapter, the role has been sub-
stantially modified, particularly in relation to older
pupils. The patterns of fear, authority, respect and coercion have largely vanished from the scene. This is the
era of the *involved* teacher, and any teacher so involved
becomes more significantly a preceptor, a catalyst and
the mainspring to new interests and new discoveries
about the self by the child.

It would seem to me that the child's self-concept is
of prime importance and interest to the teacher. The
teacher, however, must always realize that familial
conditions are paramount here. There is evidence to
suggest that children low in self-esteem have suffered
'lack of parental guidance and relatively harsh and dis-
respectful treatment' (Coopersmith, 1967), and it is
doubtful whether relationships with understanding
teachers can fully compensate in such conditions.
Thelen (1967) argues that it might be wiser to match
the teacher and pupil according to their needs, an idea
which is not without obvious attractions and advantages. In present practice, however, such 'matching'
would clearly prove an impossibility due to group and
'block' time-tabling and the existing high pupil–teacher
ratios. Social learning is particularly relevant here,
since the significance of 'models' to the developing per-

son is central to much that is in psychology. The achievement of balanced appreciation and understanding of self in relation to others is, however, a lengthy process. When we speak of maturity, particularly psychological maturity, there is a good deal of evidence to show that (as Erikson says) identity is basic to all this and that such maturity is often not reached until one's early twenties. The child, adolescent, or young adult who is maturing successfully needs amongst other things to arrive at:

1. The acceptance of self, an adjustment to appearance and ability
2. An appreciation of the individual differences of others, including their appearances and abilities
3. The recognition of role and status changes and the ability to effect these smoothly
4. An ability to meet the demands of others without undue strain
5. An achievement of a harmonious balance between the gratification, sublimation and repression of his needs and desires.

In these terms it must be remembered that much which goes for learning cannot be judged by the criteria of its worth in adult eyes but by its social value in the eyes of the peer group. Such areas listed represent major growth points both in the life of the individual and in that of the group. Even learning to accept one's appearance is by no means easy particularly for the adolescent, as has been well documented in the works of Ausubel, Fleming, McCandless, Murphy, Stolz, Stone and Church in the field of child development. In addition there is much extant in the writings of psycho-analysts to suggest that acceptance of physical appearance can be critical to a healthy self-concept. The work of Stolz and Stolz (1951) suggested that, 'at any one time or another ... about 31 per cent of the boys were definitely disturbed over physical charac-teristics such as shortness, fatness, poor physique, un-usual facial features, unusual development of the nipples, lack of muscular strength, acne, bowed legs, unusually small or large genitalia or narrow shoulders'. Twenty years ago Jones (1949) found that 41 per cent of a large sample of girls were known to suffer anxieties concerning aspects of their build, size of breasts, hair, etc. The child, and in particular the adolescent, doesn't have to be unusual to make him feel so. The resources of the mass media are often directed very consistently towards an image of seeming physical maturity and sophistication which make it hard for the late devel-oper. Fleming (1963) refers to the period of adolescence as being 'biologically determined but socially condi-tioned'. A follow-up study of the subjects investigated in the California Adolescent Studies found that as regards social acceptance the late maturer was in a less favourable position than the early maturer (Jones, 1957 and 1965). But it is interesting to note in this con-text that all the advantages are not on the side of the early maturer, since the late maturers have often had to show more flexibility and willingness to adapt their behaviour than others. This may give them some advan-tage in adulthood.

Erikson outlined eight stages in the development of the personality (1965) as follows. He suggested that the achievement of the more advanced stages of psychological maturity depended upon the preceding goals having been met successfully:

1. Infancy: a basic sense of trust
2. Early childhood: a sense of autonomy
3. Play age: a sense of initiative
4. School age: industry and competence
5. Adolescence: personal identity
6. Young adult: intimacy
7. Adulthood: generativity
8. Mature age: integrity and acceptance.

Fleming (1967) places emphasis on the importance of the self-concept in relation to learning situations and says that the most significant result of research in the field is to show that teachers should 'note the phrases and gestures which contribute to the forming of self-pictures', and remarks that, 'in response to such remarks children or adults come to think of themselves as trustworthy, responsible and competent, or unattractive, unwanted and stupid. Their behaviour tends to fall in line with their thinking'. Teachers should, I feel, take particular note of this point. Symonds (1967), drawing upon psychoanalytic concepts, says, 'To a degree the success of ego-functioning is determined by the adequacy of the self – that is the individual's concept and valuation of himself. The ego functions best when self is valued – whereas self-depreciation is usually accompanied by a falling off of the effectiveness of ego-functioning.'

As teachers, we need to ask how such a self-evaluation can be developed. If this thing is largely a product of social conditions – and it seems to be – how can teachers play a useful part? The short answer is, by making sure that our language and our relationships are both effective and affective, in order that there is a constant replenishing of the supplies of appreciation, tolerance and affection. This can probably be best achieved by ensuring aspects of success and chances for esteem whenever possible within the classroom situation. Personal identification with group and gang leaders (or for that matter with teacher), with heroes, fictional or otherwise, offers the chance of self-ideals and the possible sources of ego-strength. Ideally, it might be possible to see that identification within school is enhanced and enriched by opportunities for leaders who possess admired qualities, though, of course, this is not always practicable. (But in this respect it is possible that the prefect system does have its uses.) Books, comics, films and television all have a place to play here, though occasionally one can be horrified by the *quality* of the identification possibilities offered.

Hilgard (1967) maintains that one of the fundamentals of self-awareness is 'an evaluative judging attitude toward the self, in which the self is regarded as an object of importance, and preferably of worth'. He also points out that the self-concept needs to include information based on private experience and that continuity of memory plays a very large part in this, in that it *relates* many of our experiences and attitudes meaningfully and maintains in us an awareness of the self.

Morris (1967) stresses the importance of the relation between home and school and considers how the school can complement or compensate for the influence of the home on the child's character. Taking the question of emotional insecurity, indicated by excessive aggression or timidity, lack of concentration or unusual inhibition, he suggests that the school may help by striking a careful balance between excessive control and freedom in the classroom situation, by promoting group co-operation, especially in small-group work, and by providing teachers who, themselves mature and secure, are able to impart a sense of security to their pupils.

7

Social orientation and linguistic environment

Language development and its social implications

Language is an expression of mental processes, of information coded, stored and selected. Selected from the existing 'total' vocabulary of the culture the individual's own vocabulary is related to his interests and orientation to the material and social world in which he lives.

A considerable amount of research has been done in the field of children's language development. One of the more interesting aspects that stands out is that of the relatively high frequency with which 'I' (or 'me') occurs in a child's speech. It is noticeable that no other pronoun is normally used so readily. As early as 1931, M. E. Smith noted that over the same period of time, in a small group of children aged two to five years, 'I' appeared 2,543 times while 'you' appeared only 955 times. This is not such a trivial matter as it sounds, since it serves to illustrate that the primary matter of the child's concern is himself. This is, of course, indicated not only by the frequent use of the 'I' but by the content and tone of his remarks, questions and demands.

In 1926 Piaget published the results of his 'clinical observation' of young children, a method of observation which consisted in 'letting the child talk and in noticing the manner in which his thought unfolds itself'. He distinguished between 'egocentric' and 'socialized' speech, suggesting that in egocentric speech there is virtually no attempt to interchange ideas and that it is really a form of 'collective monologue' rather than a conversation in any sense. Socialized speech on the other hand is speech whereby the talker really tries to contact the listener, relates his utterances to the other person's viewpoint and tries to share his meanings. In Piaget's earlier work he reached the conclusion that there was little real socialized speech until the age of seven years or so. Many others, however, claim to have socialized language in children as young as three or four years, and repetitions of Piaget's methods of study have not confirmed his findings (Miller, 1951). (Other researchers, however, do not doubt the implied *sequence* of vocabulary development. Perhaps the difference between egocentric and socialized speech can be found in the willingness in the latter case to 'modify one's own utterance' in order to communicate.) The work of Vigotsky (1939) suggests that the child's speech (even the egocentric monologue) is really directed outwards towards others. Jersild (1960) resolves some of these difficulties rather obviously and caustically by saying that anyway, the more immature the child, the less chance there is of his understanding or joining in another person's point of view.

Most studies point to a connection between high socio-economic status and increased language development. Some studies, such as J. and E. Newson's (1965) amongst many others, show that parent–child inter-action is greater and more permissive in 'middle'- and professional-class families than in 'working'-class families. Certainly, one finds that longer sentences, larger vocabularies and a more complex syntactical structure are more common in the speech of children of a higher socio-economic background. These factors *might* be due in some part to higher intelligence, but, even in studies where apparent intelligence factors have been equalized, the children of the higher income groups still show a marked superiority. At any rate, a positive link is usually observable between language ability and mental ability as measured by the standard intelligence tests. But since most of such tests are based on words anyway, it is difficult to understand just what this link means. Does a child earn a high score on a verbal intelligence test because he has a good command of language, or does he have that good command of language because of his high intelligence?

Perhaps the aspect that ought to concern us more here is not so much the question of cognitive connections, but that of the social implications. Man is a talking animal who uses words to control his own behaviour and the behaviour of others. Tolman characterized speech as 'tool-behaviour' and emphasized that, as a tool, speech did not greatly differ in essence from other tools. In his book (1932) Tolman points out that speech is very like 'an extension of arms and hands and pointing apparatus'. In other words, whatever else one attributes to language, one of its main characteristics is its social utility. Communication occurs mainly through language, even in this age, and the meaning of any utterance is usually determined by relating it to the background language and category experience of the speaker and the listener. One of the commoner themes of the playwright Pinter is that of the hazards of communication between people of differing needs, attitudes and cognitions. People very often use similar words with different degrees of meaning in such a way that communication is not really possible. When my grandfather talked of 'loyalty to the firm' to his employees, his concepts and theirs of loyalty were understandably different. By 'loyalty' he meant a feeling of involvement in and love for a firm which was his creation, part of him. (Of course, he also received most of the profits.) To his employees 'loyalty' to the firm merely meant working the established stint largely for someone else's benefit.

There is, too, the apparent fact that, as well as reflecting the individual and the society, language helps to shape them. This may mean that if the language of the individual is not rich and varied, his personality may also to some extent be the less full and varied. The notion that a person's language reflects and reveals his personality is not new. Lewis refers to language as the mould or pitcher into which the fluid of the personality is poured (Lewis, 1963). Almost four hundred years ago, Ben Jonson could write, 'Speak that I may judge thee.' This may not always be a wise judge of an individual, but it is on the whole safe to assume that the language of a people or a group does usually reflect its dominant interests and concerns. This seems to hold good not only in terms of differing socio-economic background, but also in terms of fashions, trends, age groupings, loyalties, and nationalities. In an adolescent school group one can often observe a multiplicity of euphemisms all directly relating to one of the adolescent's dominant concerns – sex. T. E. Lawrence no doubt encountered a host of differing words for camel (Thomas, 1937) and many of the English public schools have their own private language (Lambert, 1968).

It seems, too, that in most societies the lower- and upper-class groups speak a different language. In England, Bernstein (1960), Lawton (1969) and others have posited that there tends to be a marked difference between the language of the poorly educated English and that of the better educated. Bernstein is one of a large number of linguists, sociologists and anthropologists who have related linguistic structure to behaviour. Among the common characteristics of the 'public' (restricted) language of the working class, he listed rigidity, simplicity, frequent-idiom and 'sympathetic circularity' (e.g. a large number of those statements or phrases which signal a requirement for the previous speech sequence to be reinforced: 'Wouldn't it?', 'You see?', 'You know', etc.). 'Accurate grammar, logical modifications and adverbs' were stated to be more characteristic of the formal (elaborated) language of the upper classes (Bernstein, 1959). There is also considerable evidence from the U.S.A. that social class is an important factor in language behaviour, verbal learning and intellectual development (see in particular the work of Jensen, 1968).

Language and cognition

The determinants of language development and intellect are very closely related to the experience of the child in the early familial environment. The influence of speech on thinking and attitude formation relates back to the development of perception and syntax in childhood. Classic experiments exist which illustrate this point and which show the part that language plays in dealing with new situations. From an early experiment Kuenne (1946) inferred that, 'Transposition to a situation not very different from a past situation may well take place without language, but language becomes more necessary as the difference increases.' In fact, most human beings seem to need language in order to deal with new situations and relationships. The question-asking behaviour of younger children later becomes an important thought 'tool' for independent problem-solving. This is not to say that language is merely the vehicle for thought, since developmentally and functionally they are both interrelated. Reference to deaf children who have restricted or retarded language development illustrates this. The comparative retardation of deaf children increases as problem-solving tests become more complex (Deutsch, *et al.*, 1968).

Whorf (1956) stated that every normal person talks and that, because of the relationship between talking and thinking, ideas are built up which are based upon concepts formed within one's own group and which may well be intolerant of any other point of view. Firth says, 'Once someone speaks to you, you are in a relatively determined context and you are not free to say just what you please. We are born individuals. But to satisfy our needs we have to become social persons, and every social person is a bundle of roles or personae, so that the situational and linguistic categories would not be unmanageable' (Lawton, 1969). Lawton, commenting on this statement of Firth's, says that, though it is relatively naive, Firth was 'certainly advancing towards an identification of speech and social structure'.

This very brief review of the literature illustrates the fact that in the formation of ideas their communication is not by any means an independent process. Language is not merely a device for voicing ideas, but rather it actually shapes them and is itself shaped as a result of interaction. We really do, as Whorf says, 'dissect nature along lines laid down by our native language'. We categorize because we want to know, but we do so according to the rules of our culture, institution and group.

A child spends a large part of its early years learning to make the correct matches between speech categories, learning to recognize all dogs and call *that animal* a dog, to differentiate between buckets and cups, scissors and shears, to relate name to object. It is interesting to note in this context that D. E. M. Gardner, writing of the Malting House School, says that Susan Isaacs found it necessary to modify the idea of Pyke's that 'every question should be referred back to the child and that children should never be told the name of anything but rather asked "Shall we call it so and so?"' Gardner says Pyke's idea tended to confuse the children. Pyke, however, 'was concerned that the children should be taught to realize that language was a convention and that words were not objects' (Gardner, 1969). Recognition and categorization are important aspects of group communication (in terms of family initially). When the child can eventually identify the referents for *words*, he can then make use of the expectancies that are shown to be operating within his group. He may expect knives to cut, dogs to bark, etc. Put differently and more crudely, he may well later come to expect the 'bosses' to behave badly and the workers to behave well, to be suspicious of teachers and 'rozzers' and so on. Indeed, language so rapidly relates to attitude formation and eventual role-playing that some social psychologists have seen fit to consider language stereotype as a major indicator for prediction of the individual's behaviour in society. Holt (1970) says:

> What we must remember about words is that they are like freight cars; they may carry a cargo of meaning, of associated non-verbal reality, or they may not. The words that enter our minds with a cargo of meaning make more complete and accurate our non-verbal model of the universe. Other words just rattle around in our heads. We may be able to spit them out, or shuffle them around according to the rules, but they have not changed what we really know and understand about things. One of the things that are so wrong with school is that most of the words children hear there carry no non-verbal meaning whatever, and so add nothing to their real understanding.

The structure of our language determines our concepts, communication and thought, but it also saves considerable amount of trouble. It acts as a useful form of second-hand experience; we can be told not to eat poisonous toadstools or to run across the road. We can learn from it as a repository of what is safe and acceptable, without ourselves having to experience danger and rejection.

The teacher and the language of the classroom

Perhaps the real question for the teacher, however, is can there be a natural or inherent antipathy in communication because of simple linguistic differences between individuals and groups? Do teachers absorb the subject style or class style and fail to communicate fully with their pupils as some of the work of Barnes (1969) would suggest? Further, is the behaviour of a person a function of the language he has acquired? Does his language thereby affect his dealings with other people or the way in which he deals with his environment? What part does the school play in the process?

It is important to remember, if one is to attempt to answer such queries, that linguistic context and concept formation are very closely linked; so closely linked that it is essential for teachers to beware of pseudo-communication in the classroom (i.e. a failure to understand fully the meaning of a communication of another person as intended, frequently without knowledge of either person). Such pseudo-communication is considerably less likely to arise in classroom climates of informality and optimum interaction. In formal co-active situations it can and very often does arise, causing unnecessary difficulties with learning and having a socially selective and divisive effect upon the class. The teacher may in fact be operating on a different linguistic wavelength from the pupils. Also, repression is a factor to consider here, since repression arises from or is associated with family interaction and is usually then maintained as part of the institutional process. Linguistic style does not seem so important here. For instance, in my own school days one of the masters could strike terror into our eleven-year-old hearts with the phrase 'Gentlemen, pray conduct yourselves with the due decorum which is expected of you.' None of us knew what it meant; we just knew that he was cross.

There is also some evidence that the assessment of pupils is in part based on language, plus looks, clothes and general compliance, particularly if these things 'fit' the assumptions held by the teacher. The central theme of *Pygmalion in the Classroom* (Rosenthal and Jacobson, 1968) is 'that one person's expectation for another's behaviour could come to serve as a self-fulfilling prophecy'.

Milner (1951), in her classic study of first-grade Negro children, stated that type and quality of the home language interaction seemed a crucial factor in early school performance. The following were more characteristic of children doing rather less well at school:

1. The children did not eat breakfast with their mothers
2. They were not able to talk with adults and only received orders
3. They did not talk with anyone between the time of finishing breakfast and leaving for school
4. They did not have any conversation with adults whilst eating supper
5. Neither their mothers nor any other adult spent much time in hugging, kissing or speaking approvingly to the children.

Eson, in *The Psychological Foundations of Education* (1964), gives a useful summary of social-class effects upon the early years of children. He says, 'The middle-class child is much more likely to have had nursery school or kindergarten experience. Also he is more likely to have received some preliminary training in communication skills.' He states that children learn different roles by virtue of different status and that such learning gives them access to and yet is partially determined by different speech systems, that Bernstein's work in particular has 'directed attention to the relations between forms of speech and forms of social relation and to the social and educational consequences of differential access to forms of speech'. This results in obviously different social and intellectual procedures and may well provide differing standpoints for members within the same school class.

The schoolchild and his language

Once a child starts school there are usually at least two distinct linguistic communities in which he will be gaining experience: that of adults and that of his friends. Lewis (1963) says that as the child grows older his early family language experiences 'tend to become submerged in certain uniformities'. These are the language of the school as a whole, the language of the peer group, the language of his sex. To most school teachers (particularly teachers in certain public schools) the language of the school is quite apparent and almost as tangible as chalk dust or the combined smell of polish, lavatories and milk. But different schools and different eras have different language fashions and customs. The borderline between the language of school, peer group, and sex is tenuous in the extreme. They are closely interrelated. Some words are encouraged by deliberate policy and institutional process as many an 'old boy' or 'old girl' will testify. 'Prep' is a good example. As preparation for further learning it has a different ring from 'homework' and suggests a more positive approach perhaps. Such words form one of the first stages of habit formation and social learning to the new school entrant.

In part, the development and the cohesion of the group depends upon the use of euphemisms, scatology, oaths, slang and a legislative code. As the Opies (1959) point out, the transmission of such a sub-language has several useful side effects, for, in addition to cohesion, and 'the code of oral legislation', it provides opportunity for the children to feel secretive, daring and independent of adults. 'The schoolchild, in his primitive community, conducts his business with his fellows by ritual declaration. His affidavits, promisory notes, claims, deeds of conveyance, receipts, and notices of resignation, are verbal and are sealed by the utterance of ancient oaths which are recognized and are considered binding by the whole community.' Sometimes an adult will deliberately foster and keep a language style which is seemingly inappropriate to his age, or keep archaic language styles alive by deliberate pedantry.

There are also in existence many sub-languages, such as those of the services, law, the church, 'old boys' clubs and secret societies, which are deliberately fostered in such a way as to provide for inclusive cohesion of members and exclusion of the general public.

Quite often children reject adult language patterns as a conscious attempt at escaping some of the adult rules of conduct. There is, too, some evidence to suggest that delinquency and linguistic inadequacy are not unrelated. But on the whole, the wish to be adult (which is usually in the ascendant during adolescence) and the socialization experience of early childhood combine to maintain the child's acceptance of adult language styles. Also, during adolescence, the membership of a sexual grouping becomes very important indeed and the distinctive vocabularies of boys and girls relate them not only to their sex, but to the physical characteristics of their sex and the sexual behaviour of adults. In this way a sort of 'verbal type-casting' takes place which reinforces role concepts and expectations. Margaret Mead suggests that the experiences of boys and girls in our culture are so different that the meanings of quite crucial words (such as 'mother', 'love', 'marriage') come to mean different things for adult men and women. She suggests that as a result of this the sexes acquire differing concepts for the same words and thereby find real communication and a common viewpoint impossible (Mead, 1962).

For the teacher, then, communication of ideas verbally is not merely the flow of information; it is much more subtle than that. It can act as the reinforcer of viewpoints or the means of group identification. It can be used in such a way as to provide clues for the instant recognition of like thinkers. It can be used to exclude others. The meaning of any utterance is determined *by the experience of the individual*. If a teacher uses a 'special' language even partly outside some or all of his class's experience, he may well induce a partial blockage in communication. The main function of such a language is to facilitate communication about matters of common interest, not to provide a host of additional constraints to the learning process.

77

Blue Umbrellas

'The thing that makes a blue umbrella with its tail—
How do you call it?' you ask. Poorly and pale
Comes my answer. For all I can call it is peacock.

Now that you go to school, you will learn how we
    call all sorts of things;
How we mar great works by our mean recital.
You will learn, for instance, that Head Monster is not
    the gentleman's accepted title;
The blue-tailed eccentrics will be merely peacocks;
    the dead bird will no longer doze
Off till tomorrow's lark, for the letter has killed him.
The dictionary is opening, the gay umbrellas close.

Oh our mistaken teachers!—
It was not a proper respect for words we need,
But a decent regard for things, those older creatures
    and more real.
Later you may even resort to writing verse
To prove the dishonesty of names and their black
    greed—
To confess your ignorance, to expiate your crime,
    seeking one spell to lift another curse.
Or you may, more commodiously, spy on your child-
    ren, busy discoveries,
Without the dubious benefit of rhyme.

D. J. ENRIGHT

8
Towards maturity: the developmental context and implications for education

Students of educational or developmental psychology soon become aware of two recurring phenomena in their studies: first and foremost that one must recognize the debt owed by psychologists and philosophers to the work of Jean Piaget over the last fifty years. The study of children's thinking would be infinitely poorer if we had not received much painstakingly gleaned information from Piaget on how children's knowledge is built up and how this can shed light on the origins of knowledge. The second, somewhat more mundane, is that care must be taken to avoid the over-enthusiastic use of chronological age as an infallible index of characteristics in children. Its merit lies in its ease of operation when dealing with approximations of normative development. Its use is inevitable, but it defeats its purpose if the wide range of individual differences is not constantly borne in mind. Very often, in order to categorize or describe, syntheses and generalizations have to be attempted. The wise student remembers, however, that usually the child reflects the home more than the school pattern (except possibly during adolescence) and that popular stereotypes can be extremely dangerous particularly if taken and applied as indications of 'correct' development.

The younger schoolchild and his acquisition of skills

Observations of teachers and research workers would lead us to believe that the child of five or thereabouts appears to reason best upon problems closest to his own experience, from personal involvement in concrete situations and as a result of optimum exposure to language skills. Usually, a child of this age is vulnerable to immediate distraction, afraid of antagonizing grown-ups, very aware of physical needs and not capable of discussions in large groups. From this it follows that wise adults dealing with groups of children of this age do not attempt to superimpose a form of social cohesiveness where it does not exist, but cater for individual attention along with the gradual promotion of awareness of others.

Neither memory nor reason is intransmutable during the early schooldays. Lies, forgetting and plain alteration of the facts to make them more palatable are all quite common. 'Inquisitions' held in class after misdemeanour are usually quite useless and suggest an ignorance of child psychology on the part of the 'inquisitor'.

Often, along with the development of skills at this age, come the concomitant problems of reversal of letters, mirror writing, failure to recognize repeated and conventional shapes, etc. Much has been written on the entering characteristics of young children when faced with reading as an information-processing skill.

Some psychologists would suggest that, by and large, five year olds see things as wholes, as Gestalten, and that in reading, early phonic instruction is largely pointless. But current developments seem to be based not only on the 'recognition of the essentially "phonic" elements in the skill of reading but more especially on a psychological analysis of the structure of the skill as a whole and its relation to language behaviour in general. Moreover, there are pitfalls to be avoided in "new style phonic" methods as there were in previous methods and these correspond to violations of the restrictions implied by the character of reading as a linguistic and representational process whose primary purpose is the acquisition of information' (Roberts and Lunzer, 1968). In general, 'method' arguments are remarkably unproductive and many infant teachers seem to be capable of success with an amalgam of early 'whole-word' methods followed by gradual phonic addition. Provided the early language is *relevant* to the child's experience, provided his *motivation* is high and provided the teacher is sensitive and committed, the average and above-average children seem to do just as well on any method or mixture of methods. With slower-learning children, there is some evidence to suggest that some phonic methods, linguistic methods and the initial teaching alphabet are having success (Reid, 1968, and Downing, 1969). There is little, however, to show that any one system is superior in every way to another, whilst there is evidence to show that home environment appears a critical factor in learning to read (Morris, 1966).

Between the ages of five and seven years, eyesight and memory seem to improve and visual perception and concentration are normally considerably enhanced. There are also noticeable increases in the skill of voluntary recall and, if these factors meet with suitable home and general influences, dispositions and motives for reading are heightened accordingly.

My own experience of seven year olds leads me to believe that they are becoming increasingly interested in the realism of the world around them. Certainly, at about this age, *small*-group work becomes more appropriate to classroom pursuits and a feeling of responsibility towards others begins to be exhibited, though the degree of group stability does seem to show different patterns for boys and girls (Northway, 1968). Opportunity for individual work and play should still be catered for at all possible times and intellectual activity needs to be planned in steady gradations so that the child may be encouraged by seeing his tangible and obvious progress. This is a stage when there is a growing interest in other children and adults. It is a stage, too, when one begins to hear and observe displays of attitudes, verbal stereotypes and social prejudices that have been encouraged or reinforced during earlier socialization experience. Much that will form the core of the adult personality is by now laid down. 'Give me the child until he is seven and I will give you the man.' At the same time it is usually the case that a gradual reticence with adults begins to show and the desire to be like others in the class, peer group and gang becomes of paramount importance. The dimensions of the child's environment are now rapidly expanding and to some extent re-alignments with peers are reinforced by cultural and institutional taboos which contribute to the drawing apart of the sexes during the following years of childhood. Though the whole part of this school stage may be thought of as largely egocentric, increasing self-assurance, the accruing of the skills of literacy, numeracy and creativity and the desire for mastery of the environment as well as self are beginning to show, moving the child outward into the more sociable years of middle latency. (Freudians and many psycho-dynamic theorists maintain that the period between roughly five to twelve years can be thought of as a period of 'latency', i.e. about the age of five or so the Oedipus complex tends to become submerged, mainly as the result of the socialization processes, and remains latent until the age when the sexual instinct is augmented by physiological change in the reproductive organs and endocrine system. Freud postulated that during this period the sexual and aggressive impulses of the child could be said to be in a *relatively* subdued state.)

The middle years of childhood and early physical maturity

Between the ages of about seven and twelve years comes a period of vigorous activity; one of the most formative periods in a human being's life. This is a period which has considerable consequence for society, since the capacity for logical thought and abstract thinking begins to grow, characters begin to settle and form, attitudes to harden, and knowledge to leap forward. Furthermore, during the years eight to twelve, adolescence begins in more than half the girls in the population and is completed by some (Marshall, 1965). Even some boys are well advanced into adolescence by the age of twelve or so. This growth, and equally important its variability, has considerable educational and social implications. The growth rate has not always been the same. Tanner (1961) states, 'Children at all ages are nowadays bigger than they were fifty or even twenty years ago. This is partly because they are growing into bigger adults, but also because they are maturing faster; a child of five now is in all physical and probably a good many psychological respects equivalent to a child of six of thirty years ago.' There is clear evidence from many parts of the world that girls are maturing at an earlier age than they used to. Both Marshall and Tanner see this as becoming progressively earlier with each generation; and Marshall says, 'The average age at which menstruation begins becomes four months earlier every ten years, so that the typical girl of today may expect to menstruate when she is about ten months younger than her mother was at the beginning of her periods' (Marshall, 1965).

This means, quite simply, that the junior-school or middle-school teacher may have to cater for the problems of the adolescent at the same time as coping with the mentally and physically underdeveloped child. Particularly large differences will exist between children of the same chronological age, and probably the most crucial diversity will occur at about the fourth-year level in the junior school (eleven years of age). As there is an undoubted relationship between level of physical maturity and the emotional and social behaviour of the child, it can be clearly seen that the mixture of extremes of development may easily result in difficulty within a class. Tanner does in fact argue that intellectual or 'social' age would be likely to produce greater homogeneity within a class than the criterion of chronological age; but he goes on to question whether it would necessarily be more worthwhile (Tanner, 1961). In all, teachers of this age group must be prepared to face an extremely complex situation, for nowadays more and more mothers go out to work and more and more parents relinquish a great deal of the responsibility for the social training of their children. Not surprisingly in these circumstances, many junior-school girls reach menarche totally unprepared. If puberty can be a source of worry and disturbance to the young teenager, how much more alarming can it be for the eight, nine or ten year old who is less well equipped by education and experience of life to be able to deal with it.

It would be foolish to over-stress the importance of early maturing, but whatever the cause – or the significance – at least no junior-school teacher should be unaware of the fact that, 'probably something between ten and twenty per cent of girls now menstruate while they are still at the primary school' (Tanner). This secular trend towards earlier maturity is not exclusive to the girls of Britain. There is considerable evidence to show that, throughout all socio-economic levels, the heights and weights of our schoolboys have increased. In fact, at all ages from seven onwards the present-day child is considerably larger than his nineteenth-century counterpart; and this trend has overridden the social class differences, so that the average boy of today is taller at all ages than the upper-class boy of the 1870s.

Both the excessively early developer and the excessively late one often feel completely estranged from the general group of children, and Tanner suggests that those who mature early often achieve an advantageous position in school right from the nursery school stage since, in terms of motor-skills, they tend to be in advance of the other children and thus to have some degree of social advantage. Particularly important is the fact that the fast-maturing child will often have a greater chance of passing any examination bound to norms of chronological age. This, coupled with the difficulty of devising techniques of age mark weighting capable of differentiating satisfactorily between the child who had received two instead of three years' infant education, must surely have contributed to the weaknesses inherent in the eleven-plus selective procedure and of streaming in the junior schools. This argument is no less applicable to streaming in the secondary schools.

At about the age of ten or eleven, most girls are on average bigger and stronger than boys of the same age. The pre-pubertal/pubertal growth spurt does therefore often ensure that the hierarchy of child power is safely in the hands of the girls in any primary school. Most primary teachers with whom I have discussed this point agree that it is in fact so. Certainly, in primary schools within my experience, each head teacher has to some extent relied upon or actively exploited the greater maturity of the older girls. This is often useful for the social life of the school, but can have the unfortunate effect of 'spoiling' the children concerned unless great care is taken. (Recent research work in the U.S.A. at the Universities of Stanford, Columbia, Harvard and at the Gesell Institute of Child Development has suggested that American elementary schools are biased in favour of girls and that it may be in part due to the fact that most elementary teachers are women, but also in part due to the greater conformity exhibited by girls – Pollack, 1968.) Certainly, in England, the primary school may well become in effect a girl-dominated community, especially if there is a prefect system, with the senior girls proving more able, more mature and more conformist than most of the boys. In such schools that I have visited, been associated with, or taught in, whether a prefect or monitorial system existed or not, the more mature girls of the school have played a predominant part. This has seemed particularly noticeable in the fields of music, art and drama; such activities often forming the cultural 'hub' of school life.

Yet, overall, the normal pre-pubertal child of late latency is busy and reliable with an even, steady mental and physical growth that makes for harmony and stability in the community life, yet encourages experiment. Such a stage of growth helps towards affectionate and warm teacher–pupil relationships, of a sort that can hardly exist at a later stage, without being detrimental to the learning of habits of concentration and perseverance. The whole atmosphere and ethos of schooling at this stage owes a great deal to the outgoing nature and level of adjustment that is commonly relevant to the seven- to eleven-year-old child.

Cognitive development

Most of the elementary schemata necessary for valid reasoning are already well within the capacity of the average child of seven; and during the four or so years which follow many children gradually develop what adults usually call logical thought, Piaget's 'formal operational thought' (Piaget and Inhelder, 1958). There is, too, a strong connection between growth in reasoning powers and the grammar learned and 'most of the school situations in which the primary-school child finds himself are verbal or contain a large verbal element' (Peel, 1960). The teacher of the seven or eight year old must be aware of the processes of thought development; must be aware too that, whereas at that age the child grasps situations involving concrete material easily, it is not so in the case of situations composed in abstract terms. At this stage the child's judgement of purely verbal problems and situations is in terms of their content and is often egocentric. But usually, by the end of the latency period, many children are beginning to be capable of the more abstract formal thought typical of the adolescent. The implication is that no teacher of this age child can afford to miss a chance to present as much concrete 'first-hand' experience as possible, allowing time for classification, serializing, discovering equivalents and carrying out substitutions. Child-centred work allowing for such individual and group activities in logical sequence requires much careful planning and is not the haphazard occurrence which some would have it be.

It is probably true to say that the better understanding of child development in England, which really owes a great deal to the work of Susan Isaacs in the 1930s, has gradually helped to change the whole atmosphere of primary education. Also, the much maligned Colleges of Education, whatever their other faults, have not been behind in exploring new avenues of approach, and the constant influx of teaching-practice students with fresh ideas frequently acts as a revitalizing factor initiating yet further points of change in the class teacher's methods. Even forty years ago the English Primary Report referred to this age of children as one when they were principally 'little workmen looking out for jobs to do' and that this was a stage when creativeness and ingenuity ought not to be stultified. Such a statement probably sounds somewhat over-sentimental to present-day students but its purport still has considerable relevance. The *critical* study of child development and thoughtful application of its insights to education has much to offer top practising teachers, though one should bear in mind Ausubel's astringent comments on the detrimental effects of developmental generalizations such as the 'internal ripening' theory of maturation (Ausubel, 1968).

During the latter half of the latency period most children seem to have developed at the interpersonal level a 'sense of justice' which enables them quite competently to choose their own group leaders and to see that the group functions reasonably well. Helen Parkhurst (of Dalton Plan fame) did in fact come to the conclusion that individual work was neither wise nor suitable at this age in anything other than short periods. Obviously though, a lot depends upon the context of the learning and the environment, and both should be taken into account in the planning of a style of approach appropriate to an individual child.

However, confidence in the essential 'fairness' of the late latency stage does not mean unlimited confidence in systems of organization within institutions which allow for unwarranted power by some children over others. It is a mistake to extrapolate from the ten-year-old group working in harmony a position which equates them with a full understanding of adult values. Generally speaking, this is a stage when resolutions may be high, but the ability to sustain the concentration needed for follow-through fluctuates enormously.

Latency seems, too, to be an age when personalities intrigue the children and when identification and introjection are constantly taking place. By this I mean that, within my experience, children of this age are very fond of ascribing to inanimate objects the characteristics of living creatures, as well as continually absorbing into themselves models and characteristics of those who attract or work with them. It follows from this that children at this stage are beginning to direct their attention outwards towards others in terms of their own social and emotional growth and becoming intensely interested in heroes, explorers, comic-strip characters, television personalities, etc.

Parallel with 'direction outwards' in terms of personalities comes the curiosity over construction. This seems to gather strength during latency to become an intense interest in finding out how things work in spheres of both animate and inanimate objects. Acting, too, is often very popular at this stage and free and formal drama combine well with group cohesiveness and identification and introjection processes, as well as having almost unlimited possibilities for the release of tension and the (often unconscious) working out of problems.

Late latency is certainly the stage of the club, the gang and the collector. Whether it is an age of sexual curiosity is a matter of some debate. It does appear to be a period of advanced but *uninvolved* sexual curiosity; a period of interest without those concomitant catalysts of adolescence, physical change, self-observation and increased auto-eroticism. Paradoxically, it also seems to be a stage when boys and girls will often play together on relatively equal terms. Group cohesiveness might well be interpreted as *conformity*, too, since attention to the demands of the peer group becomes very strong indeed. This conformity frequently shows itself in the dislike of too much affection display by parents, particularly in front of friends, though from even the ten or eleven year old there is still the occasional spontaneous outburst of affection more reminiscent of earlier childhood. Above all, later latency is a stage when fights and games are enjoyable and therapeutic and when fantasy provides models and inner possibilities for development and the resolution of problems. (Note that physiologically the latency period is one of the most healthy of our lives, though injury from accident is relatively common. The very wide variation in the maturation rates of children should always be borne in mind.)

Adolescence: reflections of self and the developing personality

Western societies appear to see adolescence as a clearly separable and definitive stage in personality formation and one brought about by biological changes, notably the onset of puberty, and critically influenced by cultural expectations. Genetic, neuro-endocrine, nutritional and social-psychological factors all combine to provide the host of variables which contribute to the change from child to adult. Certainly, the psychological impact upon the personality of bodily change and the accompanying changes in social expectations can present a bewildering set of possibilities to the pubertal child, particularly when visible discrepancies are extant culturally and even locally and when differences between adult behaviour and adolescent behaviour can seem so subtle or so meaningless. Exploratory behaviour, conflicts and constant reassessments of self-image naturally take place and problems of identification with others may become acute. Possibilities for adult role-playing experiences occur more frequently and, with them, the thirteen or fourteen year old can begin to move away from his derived status of dependency upon parents. The peer group becomes increasingly more important as a general rule and emulation of revered peers and remote adult models is frequent.

One of the problems inherent in a technico-industrial society is its demands upon mass education and the necessary prolongation of an adolescent 'in-between status', especially for the middle-class or aspiring middle-class youth. Another problem is that of the psycho-sexual acquisition of firm sex-roles which relate to childhood concepts of masculinity and femininity and yet make sense in terms of contemporary physical and socio-cultural expectations. Another is that probably, as Erikson says, adolescence in our present age has been over-diagnosed as a crisis period to the point where a 'crisis role-set' is almost deliberately set up and many react accordingly.

Very few arbitrary assemblies of adolescents, such as a class of fourteen year olds, can be said to constitute a homogeneous group, since the difference in physique, in levels of intellectual, social and emotional maturity will be so marked. In consequence assumptions regarding 'norms' are even less reliable than in earlier childhood.

Nevertheless, it is safe to assume that adolescence *is* a period when increased sensitivity is marked and when social standing and autonomy become issues of crucial importance. Real or imagined attacks upon prestige can be opposed violently and rapid changes in temperament and attitude are commonly observable. Generally speaking, during adolescence, sulking constitutes a normal reaction to frustration and there is some evidence to suggest that this is due to the attempts by adolescents to restrict more overt expressions of temper and physical violence. Most parents and teachers are familiar with the day-dreaming, 'mooning' adolescent sitting or wandering aimlessly, half lost in a private world. Too often there are real fears connected with maturation. The individual is usually very aware of physical development, terrified of becoming an oddity or just different, frightened that there is something abnormal about the sex organs; factors in the growth process that are by no means trivial, since it should be remembered that from such feelings of being too fat, too thin, sexually unattractive, unusually hairy or hairless can spring some of the crushing inferiority feelings of adulthood. Research shows that preoccupation with own bodies rates highly, closely followed by fears connected with loss of status in the peer group or loss of social standing.

Freud referred to the final stage in the developing personality as the genital stage, a stage characterized by object choices which lead to a completeness of self-concept and aceptance of adult responsibilities. Physiological changes during adolescence imply constant reassessment of self in relation to others, the possibilities of role confusion and the problems of ego-identity. Erikson says, 'The adolescent mind is essentially a mind of the moratorium, a psycho-social stage between child-hood and adulthood, and between the morality learned by the child and the ethics to be developed by the adult. It is an ideological mind – and, indeed, it is the ideological outlook of a society that speaks most clearly to the adolescent who is eager to be affirmed by his peers, and is ready to be confirmed by rituals, creeds and programmes which at the same time define what is evil, uncanny and inimical' (Erikson, 1965).

Developing sexual tensions contribute to the feelings of belonging to two worlds, the feelings of dependency on parents yet of autonomy and possibility of action as an independent social unit. This transition stage, both of intellect and emotion, is in part affected by the cul-ture or sub-culture in which the adolescent is immersed. Outlets for affections and loyalties are constantly needed, and it is wise for parents and teachers to re-member that adolescence may well be punctuated by a series of crushes for members of the same or opposite sex. It is probably true to say that in Western culture the main outlet for affection used to be in the widening of group loyalties and in the crushes which develop at this stage. But with the more permissive trends in our society, implicit and sometimes explicit encourage-ment of overtly sexual exploration is such that a con-siderable number of youngsters form liaisons with the opposite sex quite early in adolescence.

Ego-ideals often clash with family or school loyalties. The family sometimes does not approve of the adoles-cent's friends and puts pressure upon the adolescent to end relationships and occupations that seem to run con-trary to the family's or culture's predominant socializa-tion interests. A good deal of adolescent affection finds

94

its outlet in the group or gang life that is wearily toler-
ated by parents and teachers rather than actively con-
doned. (The term 'gang' is traditionally used to refer to
lower-class peer groups. 'Clique' is more often used for
upper- and middle-class peer groups, especially in the
U.S.A. Probably the best single study of cliques is found
in Hollingshead, 1949). Were such adolescent activities
fully approved of by elders, they would of course lose
much of their appeal and purpose for these youngsters.
It would appear that, though security is of prime importance to the well-being of the developing human, it
must at this stage be felt to exist in the background
rather than openly observed.

A useful comment to bear in mind is that of McFarland (1969). He says, 'It is difficult to decide whether
adolescents differ markedly in character from one generation to another or whether psychologists have to
keep themselves in a job by inventing new models of
adolescence from generation to generation.' Before
reaching full maturity presumably all human beings
attempt to establish a positive ego-identity. The self-
reflections in part necessary for this establishment are
closely connected to the norms and *mores* of the prevailing culture or sub-culture. Thus from generation to
generation different emphases, life styles and fashions
bring accompanying changes which show themselves as
'problems' at nodal development points in the growth
process. Adults may in all probability best understand
the turbulent situations of adolescence by appreciating
the adolescent *as a person* rather than placing excessive
emphasis upon the context of the situation; and as a
person he will need acceptance, the opportunity to give
and receive affection, status in the peer group, pos-

sibilities for real exploration and adventure (including sexual exploration) and the chance to make sense of the world around him.

Those concepts of social ideals and social justice which have been emerging during latency at the inter-personal level gain a far greater significance with the gradual growth of formal reasoning at the age of twelve or so. Piaget and Inhelder (1969) say, 'The pos-sibilities opened up by these new values are obvious in the adolescent, who differs from the child in that he is not only capable of forming theories but is also con-cerned with choosing a career that will permit him to satisfy his need for social reform and for new ideas.' The process of acquiring a sense of personal identity which is the major task of adolescence and which is acquired largely through social interaction is a concomi-tant of expanding and changing values. Indeed, the adolescent may frequently discover that adults are cap-able of misrepresentation and that 'parents do not always "tell it like it is" ' (Medinnus and Johnson, 1968). Intellectual development has gradually bestowed the completion of reflective thought and the adolescent's re-flections and probings may not always be for the com-fort of his elders. (But it should be pointed out that in developmental psychology there are a large number of theorists who, opposing Piaget, claim that most of human intellectual growth occurs well prior to adol-escence and that Piaget's statements concerning qualita-tive changes in intellectual functioning during adoles-cence are not borne out by other studies (Bloom, 1964).

The education of adolescents

In England until the 1950s the provision of education for adolescents was frequently socially divisive, and in many instances it still is. Whatever the advantages were of the old secondary modern school (and many were good schools with dedicated staff and imaginative curricula) it cannot have been useful for the adolescent self-image to have been conscious of rejection at such an early stage in life. Since then, the spread of comprehensive education has done much to prevent too early a social stratification and has to some extent removed unnecessary pressures from both the primary-school child and the twelve to fifteen year old, as well as allowing in part for greater flexibility of curricula. But are the schools yet meeting the needs of adolescents? Since the state secondary school is a public institution, it should logically serve the needs of all adolescents, or at least some 94 per cent of them in England. (Approximately 6 per cent of them attend private institutions.) It should be a place of relevance, challenge and excitement, not a place of dullness and conformity; and since adolescence is a period of becoming adult, such an institution should provide the individual with opportunity for observation and criticism of adult values, interaction with adults and peers, and the chance to 'try on' new behaviour. There are signs that give grounds for some optimism. The massive injection of ideas, research and know-how from the Schools Council has done much to help the situation; not least because it is a body not of experts advising from outside but one composed of practising educationists and teachers from all levels of the system. It has commissioned outside agencies (such as

97

the N.F.E.R. and Institutes of Education) to undertake a wide variety of investigations into such matters as curriculum, the development of new projects, the relations between parents and school, school organization, attitudes of students, reliability of exams, etc. There has also been a radical change in the approach to secondary-school organization over the last decade or so, with a higher degree of participation in decision-making by the children and staff, a breakdown of subject barriers, and the introduction of flexible systems of setting and non-streaming; all of which lead to a greater feeling of involvement on the part of the children and make the school more relevant to their needs. Election of sixth-formers on to the governing body of the school has already taken place. There has also been a considerable growth in forms of education with a 'college approach' to study and more fitted to the needs of older adolescents; and some of these sixth-form colleges and county colleges offer possibilities of greater independence, freedom and self-reliance to the participating student. Another of the exciting and rapid growth points has been the adoption by state schools of 'Outward Bound' type schemes and the adaptation and variety of other challenging opportunities that have arisen as a result. Contact with parents also seems to be improving; a critical factor in relation to early leaving as the Schools Council Enquiry No. 1 pointed out. It is also less common to hear of schools without a P.T.A. or to see notices requesting parents not to enter the school without an appointment. Two-way reports are becoming more common and many more schools enlist parental help with outings and school journeys and matters other than fund-raising ventures.

Overall, there are interesting signs that the adult culture is beginning to provide more opportunities for the adolescent to prove his competence and establish self-understanding. If this trend can be continued and if schools can see it as one of their prime tasks to work *with* children and adolescents we may perhaps eventually emerge from the situation where to the majority of youth institutionalized education has appeared largely irrelevant.

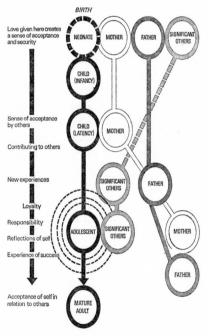

Fig. 2 *The developing person's needs and relationships* (note the way that significant others move to a position of central influence during adolescence)

Bibliography

ABERCROMBIE, M. L. JOHNSON, 1960, *The Anatomy of Judgement*, Hutchinson.

ANDERSON, H. H., *et al.*, 1945 and 1946, 'Dominative and integrative features of teachers' personalities', *Applied Psychology Monographs*, nos. 6, 8 and 11.

ASCH, S. E., 1960, 'Effects of group pressure upon modification and distortion of judgements', in Cartwright, D., and Zander, A., *Group Dynamics: Research and Theory* (2nd edn), Tavistock.

AUSUBEL, D. P., 1968, 'Viewpoints from related disciplines: Human Growth and Development', in Evans, E. D. (ed.), *Children: Readings in Behaviour and Development*, Holt, Rinehart & Winston, N.Y.

BALES, R. F., 1951, *Interaction Process Analysis*, Addison Wesley, Cambridge, Mass.

BALLER, W. R., and CHARLES, D. C., 1968, *The Psychology of Human Growth and Development* (2nd edn), Holt, Rinehart & Winston, N.Y.

BANKS, O., 1968, *The Sociology of Education*, Batsford.

BANTOCK, G. H., 1967, *Education, Culture and the Emotions*, Faber & Faber.

BARNES, D., 1969, *Language, the Learner and the School*, Penguin Books.

BELLACK, A., *et al.*, 1966, *The Language of the Classroom*, T.C. Columbia, N.Y.

BERNSTEIN, B., 1959, 'A public language: some sociological determinants of linguistic form', *The British Journal of Sociology*, vol. 10.

BERNSTEIN, B., 1960, 'Language and social class', *The British Journal of Sociology*, vol. 11.

BERNSTEIN, B., 1961, 'Social structure, language and learning', *Educational Research*, vol. 3.

BIDDLE, B., *et al.*, 1961 and 1962, *Studies in the Role of the Public School Teacher*, 5 vols, University of Missouri Research Monographs, Columbia.

BIDWELL, C., 1965, 'The school as a formal organisation', in March, J. G. (ed.), *Handbook of Organisations*, Rand McNally, Chicago.

BION, W. R., 1963, *Experience in Groups*, Tavistock.

BLOOM, B. S., 1964, *Stability and Change in Human Characteristics*, Wiley, N.Y.

BLOS. P., 1941, *The Adolescent Personality*, Appleton-Century-Crofts, N.Y.

BLYTH, W. A. L., 1965, *English Primary Education*, vols 1 and 2, Routledge & Kegan Paul.

BOWLBY, J., *et al.*, 1966, *Maternal Care*, Schocken, N.Y.

BURT, C., 1945 (February), 'The education of illiterate adults', *British Journal of Educational Psychology*, vol. 15.

BUSH, R. N., 1954, *The Teacher–Pupil Relationship*, Prentice-Hall, New Jersey.

BUTCHER, H. J., (ed.), 1968, *Educational Research in Britain*, University of London Press.

CARTER, L. F., *et al.*, 1951, 'The relations of categorisations and ratings in the observation of group behaviour', *Human Relations*, no. 4.

CARTWRIGHT, D., and ZANDER, A., 1960, *Group Dynamics: Research and Theory* (2nd edn), Tavistock.

CENTRAL ADVISORY COUNCIL FOR EDUCATION (England), 1967, *Children and Their Primary Schools* (Plowden Report), H.M.S.O.

CHINOY, E., 1954, *Sociological Perspective*, Random House, N.Y.

CHRISTENSEN, C. M., 1960, 'Relationship between pupil achievement, pupil affect-need, teacher warmth and teacher permissiveness', *Journal of Educational Psychology*, no. 51.

COHEN, L., 1965, 'An exploratory study of the teacher's role as perceived by headteacher, tutors and students in a training college', unpublished M.Ed. thesis, University of Liverpool.

COLEMAN, J. S., 1961, *The Adolescent Society*, The Free Press, N.Y.

CONNELL, W. F., DEBUS, R. L., and NIBLETT, W. R., 1967, *Readings in the Foundations of Education*, Routledge & Kegan Paul.

COOLEY, C. H., 1909, *Social Organisation*, Scribner, N.Y.

COOPERSMITH, S., 1967, *The Antecedents of Self-Esteem*, Freeman & Co., San Francisco.

COSER, L. A., and ROSENBERG, B, (eds), 1966, *Sociological Theory*, Collier–Macmillan, N.Y.

CRONBACH, L., 1961, *Essentials of Psychological Testing*, (2nd edn), Harper & Row, N.Y.

CRUTCHFIELD, R. S., 1955, 'Conformity and character', *American Psychology*, vol. 10.

DEARDEN, R., 1968, *The Philosophy of Primary Education*, Routledge & Kegan Paul.

DE CECCO, J. P., 1967, *The Psychology of Language, Thought and Instruction*, Holt, Rinehart & Winston.

DENTLER, R. A., and MACKLER, B., 1962, 'Mental ability and sociometric status among retarded children', *Psychological Bulletin*, no. 59.

DEUTSCH, M., 1960, 'The effects of cooperation and competition upon the group process', in Cartwright, D., and Zander, A., *Group Dynamics: Research and Theory* (2nd edn), Tavistock.

DEUTSCH, M., KATZ, I., and JENSEN, A. R., 1968, *Social Class, Race and Psychological Development*, Holt, Rinehart & Winston, N.Y.

DIACK, H., 1965, *In Spite of the Alphabet*, Chatto & Windus.

DOTTRENS, R., 1962, *The Primary School Curriculum*, UNESCO.

DOWNING, J., 1969, 'i.t.a. and slow learners: a reappraisal', in *Educational Research*, vol. 11 (June).

DRUCKER, P., 1959, *Landmarks of Tomorrow*, Harper, N.Y.

ELKIN, F., 1960, *The Child and Society*, Random House, N.Y.

ENRIGHT, D. J., 1968, *Selected Poems*, Chatto & Windus.

ERIKSON, E., 1958, *Young Man Luther*, Norton, N.Y.

ERIKSON, E., 1965, *Childhood and Society* (rev. edn), Hogarth Press.

ERIKSON, E., 1968, *Identity, Youth and Crisis*, Faber & Faber.

ESON, M. E., 1964, *Psychological Foundations of Education*, Holt, Rinehart & Winston, N.Y.

EVANS, K. M., 1961, 'An annotated bibliography of British Research on teaching and teaching ability', *Educational Research*, vol. 4, no. 1.

BIBLIOGRAPHY

EVANS, K. M., 1967, 'Teacher training courses and students' personal qualities', *Educational Research*, vol. 10, no. 1.

FARIS, E., 1937, *The Nature of Human Nature*, McGraw Hill, N.Y.

FESTINGER, L., and ARONSON, E., 1960, 'The arousal and reduction of dissonance in social contexts', in Cartwright, D., and Zander, A., *Group Dynamics: Research and Theory* (2nd edn), Tavistock.

FLEMING, C. M., 1959, *The Social Psychology of Education* (2nd rev. edn), Routledge & Kegan Paul.

FLEMING, C. M., 1963, *Adolescence: its social psychology* (2nd rev. edn), Routledge & Kegan Paul.

FLEMING, C. M., 1967, 'The contribution of the self concept to education', in Connell, W. F., Debus, R. L., and Niblett, W. R., *Readings in the Foundations of Education*, Routledge & Kegan Paul.

FLOUD, J., 1962, 'Teaching in the affluent society', *The British Journal of Sociology*, vol. 13.

FLOUD, J., and SCOTT, 1961, in Halsey, A. H. Floud, J., and Anderson, C. A., *Education, Economy and Society*, Free Press, N.Y.

FREUD, S., 1921, *Group Psychology and the Analysis of the Ego*, Allen & Unwin.

GAGE, N. L., (ed.), 1963, *Handbook of Research on Teaching*, Rand McNally, Illinois.

GAMMAGE, P., 1967, 'The perception of the social role of primary school teachers by parents, pupils and teachers', unpublished M.Ed. thesis, Leicester Univ.

GARDNER, D. E. M., 1969, *Susan Isaacs: The First Biography*, Methuen.

GREEN, L., 1968, *Parents and Teachers*, Allen & Unwin.

HARGREAVES, D. H., 1967, *Social Relations in a Secondary School*, Routledge & Kegan Paul.

HILGARD, E. R., 1967, 'Human motives and the concept of self', in Lazarus, R. S., and Opton, E. M. (eds), *Personality*, Penguin Books.

HOLLINGSHEAD, A. B., 1949, *Elmtown's Youth*, Wiley, N.Y.

HOLT, H., 1970, *The Underachieving School*, Pitman.

HOMANS, G. C., 1951, *The Human Group*, Routledge & Kegan Paul.

HOYLE, E., 1969, *The Role of the Teacher*, Routledge & Kegan Paul.

I.L.E.A., 1969, *Report on the Use of the Initial Teaching Alphabet in a Sample of London Schools (1963-7)*, I.L.E.A., London.

JENKINS, D., 1966, *The Educated Society*, Faber & Faber.

JENNINGS, H. H., 1943, *Leadership and Isolation*, Longmans, Green & Co., N.Y.

JENNINGS, H. H., 1959, *Sociometry in Group Relations*, American Council on Education, Washington.

JENSEN, A. R., 1967, 'The culturally disadvantaged', in *Educational Research*, vol. 10, no. 1.

JENSEN, A. R., 1968, 'Social class and verbal learning', in Deutsch, M., Katz, I., and Jensen, A. R. (eds), *Social Class, Race, and Psychological Development*, Holt, Rinehart & Winston, N.Y.

JENSEN, A. R., 1969, 'How much can we boost I.Q. and scholastic achievement?', in *Harvard Educational Review*, winter.

JERSILD, A. T., 1955, *When Teachers Face Themselves*, T.C. Columbia, N.Y.

JERSILD, A. T., 1960, *Child Psychology* (5th edn), Staples Press.

JONES, H. E., 1949, *Development of Adolescents*, Appleton Century, N.Y.

JONES, H. E., 1960, 'The longitudinal method on the study of personality' in Iscoe, I., and Stevenson, H. (eds), *Personality Development in Children*, University of Texas Press, Austin, Texas.

JONES. M. C., 1957, 'The later careers of boys who were early or late maturers', in *Child Development*, no. 28.

JONES, M. C., 1965, in *Child Development*, no. 36.

KERKMAN. D. H., and WRIGHT, H. F., 1961, *A Cinematographic Study of Classroom Behavior Patterns*, paper presented to the A.P.A. in 1961 and published that year.

KERR, C., 1963, *The Uses of the University*, Harvard University Press, Cambridge, Mass.

KING-HALL, R., HANS, N., and LAUWERYS, J. A. (eds), 1953, 'The social position of teachers', *The Year Book of Education*, 1953, Evans Bros.

KLEIN, J., 1956, *The Study of Groups*, Routledge & Kegan Paul.

KUENNE, M. R., 1946, 'An experimental investigation of the relation of language to transpositional behaviour in young children', in *Journal of Experimental Psychology*, vol. 36.

LAMBERT, R., 1968, *The Hothouse Society*, Weidenfeld & Nicolson.

LAWTON, D., 1969, *Social Class, Language and Education*, Routledge & Kegan Paul.

LAZARUS, R. S., and OPTON, E. M. (eds), 1967, *Personality*, Penguin Books.

LEBOVICI, S., 1966, 'The concept of maternal deprivation', in Bowlby, J., *et al.*, *Maternal Care*, Schocken, N.Y.

LEWIS, M. M., 1953, *The Importancy of Illiteracy*, Harrap.

LEWIS, M. M., 1963, *Language, Thought and Personality in Infancy and Childhood*, Harrap.

LUNZER, E. A., and MORRIS, J. F., 1968, *Development in Human Learning*, 2, Staples Press.

LUNZER, E. A., and MORRIS, J. F., 1969, *Contexts of Education*, 3, Staples Press.

MARSHALL, W. A., 1965, 'Childhood', in *The Seven Ages of Man, New Society* publication, London.

MCCANDLESS, B. R., 1969, *Children, Behavior and Development* (2nd edn), Holt, Rinehart & Winston, N.Y.

MCCANDLESS, B. R., BILOUS, C. B., and BENNETT, H. L., 1961, 'Peer popularity and dependence on adults in pre-school age socialization', *Child Development*, no. 32.

MCFARLAND, H. S. W., 1969, *Human Learning: a developmental analysis*, Routledge & Kegan Paul.

MCMULLEN, I., 1969, 'The identity of the teacher', in Taylor, W. (ed.), *Towards a Policy for the Education of Teachers*, Colston Papers, no. 20, Butterworth.

MEAD, M., 1962, *Male and Female*, Penguin Books.

MEDINNUS, G. R., and JOHNSON, R. C., 1968, *Child and Adolescent Psychology*, Wiley, N.Y.

MERTON, R. K., 1957, 'The Role Set: Problems in Sociological Theory', in *The British Journal of Sociology*, vol. 8, no. 2.

MILLER, G. A., 1951, *Language and Communication*, McGraw Hill, N.Y.

MILNER, E., 1951, 'A study of the relationships between reading readiness in Grade 1 school children and patterns of parent-child interaction', in *Child Development*, vol. 22.

MITCHELL, G. DUNCAN, 1968, *A Dictionary of Sociology*, Routledge & Kegan Paul.

MORRIS, B. S., 1965, 'How does a group learn to work together?', in Niblett, W. R. (ed.), *How and Why do we Learn?*, Faber & Faber.

MORRIS, B. S., 1967, 'An outline of normal development', in Connell, W. F., Debus, R. L., and Niblett, W. R. (eds), *Readings in the Foundations of Education*, Routledge & Kegan Paul.

MORRIS, B. S., 1967, 'Towards mental health in school', in Connell, Debus and Niblett, *op. cit.*

MORRIS, J. M., 1966, *Standards and Progress in Reading*, Research Report, 2nd series, no. 1, N.F.E.R.

MOUSTAKAS, C. E., 1956, *The Teacher and The Child*, McGraw Hill, N.Y.

MUSGROVE, F., and TAYLOR, P. H., 1969, *Society and the Teacher's Role*, Routledge & Kegan Paul.

MUSSEN, P. H. (ed.), 1960, *Handbook of Research Methods in Child Development*, Wiley, N.Y.

NEWCOMB, T. M., 1960, 'Varieties of interpersonal attraction', in Cartwright, D., and Zander, A., *Group Dynamics: Research and Theory* (2nd edn), Tavistock.

NEWSON, J., and NEWSON, E., 1965, *Patterns of Infant Care*, Penguin Books.

NIBLETT, W. R. (ed.), 1965, *How and Why do we Learn?*, Faber & Faber.

NORTHWAY, M. L., 1953, *A Primer of Sociometry*, University of Toronto, Toronto.

NORTHWAY, M. L., 1968, 'The stability of young children's social relations', in *Educational Research*, vol. 11.

OESER, O. A. (ed.), 1955, *Teacher, Pupil and Task*, Tavistock.

OPIE, I., and OPIE, P., 1959, *The Lore and Language of Schoolchildren*, Oxford University Press.

OTTAWAY, A. K. C., 1962, *Education and Society* (2nd rev. edn), Routledge & Kegan Paul.

PARSONS, T., and SHILS, E. A., 1952, *Toward a General Theory of Action*, Harvard University Press, Cambridge, Mass.

PEEL, E. A., 1956, *The Psychological Basis of Education*, Oliver & Boyd.

PEEL, E. A., 1960, *The Pupil's Thinking*, Oldbourne.

PIAGET, J., 1926, *The Language and Thought of the Child*, Routledge.

PIAGET, J., and INHELDER, B., 1958, *The Growth of Logical Thinking*, Routledge & Kegan Paul.

PIAGET, J., and INHELDER, B., 1969, *The Psychology of the Child*, Routledge & Kegan Paul.

POLLACK, J. M., 1968, 'Are teachers fair to boys?', in *Today's Health* (April), U.S.A.

REID, J. F., 1968, 'Reading', in Butcher, H. J. (ed.), *Educational Research in Britain*, University of London Press.

RICHARDSON, J. E., 1967, *Group Study for Teachers*, Routledge & Kegan Paul.

RIDL, F., and WATTENBERG, W., 1951, *Mental Hygiene in Teaching*, Harcourt Brace, N.Y.

ROBERTS, and LUNZER, E. A., 1968, in Lunzer, E. A., and Morris, J. F., *Development in Human Learning*, 2, Staples Press.

ROSENTHAL, R., and JACOBSON, L., 1968, *Pygmalion in the Classroom*, Holt, Rinehart & Winston, N.Y.

ROSENTHAL, R., and JACOBSON, L., 1968, 'Self-fulfilling

prophecies in the classroom', in Deutsch, M., Katz, I., and Jensen, A. R. (eds), *Social Class, Race and Psychological Development*, Holt, Rinehart & Winston, N.Y.

RUNKEL, P. J., 1956, 'Cognitive similarity in facilitating communication', in *Sociometry*, no. 19.

RYANS, D. G., 1961, 'Characteristics of teachers', *Journal of Educational Psychology*, no. 52.

SANFORD, A. (ed.), 1962, *The American College*, Wiley, N.Y.

SCHOOLS COUNCIL, 1968, *Young School-leavers*, Enquiry no. 1, H.M.S.O.

SHERIF, M., and CANTRIL, H., 1947, *The Psychology of Ego-involvements*, Wiley, N.Y.

SHILS, E. A., 1951, 'The study of the primary group', in Lerner, D., and Lasswell, H. D., *The Policy Sciences*, Stanford University Press.

SIMMEL, G., 1966, 'The dyad and the triad', in Coser, L. A., and Rosenberg, B., (eds), *Sociological Theory*, Collier–Macmillan, N.Y.

SIMON, B., (ed.), 1964, *Non Streaming in the Junior School*, P.S.W. Publications, Leicester.

SMITH, M. E., 1931, 'A study of five bilingual children from the same family', *Child development*, no. 2.

SPROTT, W. J. H., 1958, *Human Groups*, Penguin Books.

STERN, G. G., 1962, 'Environment for learning', in Sanford, A. (ed.), *The American College*, Wiley, N.Y.

STOLZ, H. R., and STOLZ, L. M., 1951, *Somatic Development of Adolescent Boys*, Macmillan, N.Y.

STONE, L. J., and CHURCH, J., 1965, *Childhood and Adolescence* (2nd edn.), Random House, N.Y.

STOTT, D. H., 1950, *Delinquency and Human Nature*, Carnegie U.K. Trust.

STOUFFER, S. A., *et al.*, 1949, 'Combat and its aftermath', in *The American Soldier*, vol. 11, Oxford University Press.

SYMONDS, P. M., 1967, 'The child's evaluation of himself as the basis for mental health', in Connell, W. F., Debus, R. L., and Niblett, W. R., *Readings in the Foundations of Education*, Routledge & Kegan Paul.

TANNER, J. M., 1961, *Education and Physical Growth*, University of London Press.

TAYLOR, W. (ed.), 1969, *Towards a Policy for the Education of Teachers*, Butterworth.

THELEN, H. A., 1967, *Classroom Grouping for Teachability*, Wiley, N.Y.

THIBAUT, J. W., and KELLEY, H. H., 1959, *The Social Psychology of Groups*, Wiley, N.Y.

THOMAS, W. I., 1937, *Primitive Behavior: An Introduction to the Social Sciences*, McGraw Hill, N.Y.

TOLMAN, E. C., 1932, *Purposive Behavior in Animals and Men*, Century, N.Y.

TROPP, A., 1956, *The School Teachers*, Heinemann.

TROW, W. C., ZANDER, A., and MORSE. W. C., 1950, 'The class as a group', in *Journal of Educational Psychology*, 41.

VERNON, P. E., 1953, 'The psychological traits of teachers', in King-Hall, R., Hans, N., and Lauwerys, J. A., *The Year Book of Education, 1953*, Evans Bros.

VIGOTSKY, L. S., 1939, 'Thought and speech', *Psychiatry*, no. 2.

WALL, W. D., 1948, *The Adolescent Child*, Methuen.

WASHBURNE, C., and HEIL, L. M., 1960, 'What characteristics of teachers affect children's growth', in *School Review*, no. 68.

WATTS, A. F., 1944, *The Language and Mental Development of Children*, Harrap.

WESTWOOD, L. J., 1967, 'The role of the teacher', in *Educational Research*, vol. 9, no. 2, and vol. 10, no. 1.

WHITE, R., and LIPPITT, R., 1960, 'Leader behavior and member reaction in three social climates', in Cartwright, D., and Zander, A., *Group Dynamics: Research and Theory* (2nd edn), Tavistock.

WHORF, B. L., 1956, *Language, Thought and Reality* (ed. by Carroll, J. B.), Wiley, N.Y.

WHYTE, W. F., 1943, *Street Corner Society, The Social Structure of an Italian Slum*, University of Chicago Press.

WILSON, B. R., 1962, 'The teacher's role', *The British Journal of Sociology*, vol, 13, no. 1.

WISEMAN, S., 1965, 'Learning versus teaching', in Niblett, W. R. (ed.), *How and Why do we Learn?'*, Faber & Faber.

WITHALL, J., 1951, 'The development of the climate index', in *Journal of Educational Research*, no. 45.

Suggestions for further reading

A. Recent works in the sociology and social-psychology of education

BANKS, O., *Sociology of Education*, Batsford, 1968.
A major introductory textbook to the sociology of education which deals clearly with sociological concepts, is stimulating reading and which contains many well-documented references.

BLYTH, W. A. L., *English Primary Education*, 2 vols., Routledge & Kegan Paul, 2nd edn, 1967, now in paperback.
These two volumes would be essential reading for any serious student of English primary education. Volume One contains an analysis of social structure and processes at the various stage levels of the primary school. Volume Two consists of a variety of essays on the middle years of childhood, on traditions in English primary education, the social context of the child's world outside school and on the school in relation to local environment and wider society.

GUSKIN, A. E. and GUSKIN, S. L., *A Social Psychology of Education*, Addison-Wesley, Reading, Mass. 1970.
This book focuses mainly upon interpersonal relations in American schools. Educational roles are amplified in terms of requirements and expectations rather than in terms of personality factors. Achieve-

ment orientation and the connections between educational aspiration and primary socialization are also dealt with. There is a brief discussion on the roles of teacher, pupil and school administrator.

HOYLE, E., *The Role of the Teacher*, Routledge & Kegan Paul, 1969.
A small but very thorough summary and study guide to the role of the teacher. The discussion on the role in an advanced technological society is particularly useful and well documented.

LAWTON, D., *Social Class, Language and Education*, Routledge & Kegan Paul, 1968.
A very important book in the field of education. It deals with the difficulties of working-class pupils at school and of the problems of differential access to educational opportunity. Language development and usage are fully discussed and there is a fairly comprehensive critique of much of Bernstein's earlier work.

LUNZER, E. A., and MORRIS, J. F. (ed.), *Development in Learning*, vol. 3, 'Contexts of Education', Staples Press, 1968.
This is one of three volumes in a comprehensive set of readings on the acquisition of knowledge and of the skills and techniques appropriate to schooling. It covers two broadly related topics: the part played in learning by individual differences and a general analysis of social factors in education.

MORRISON, A., and MCINTYRE, D., *Teachers and Teaching*, Penguin Books, 1969.
An attempt to relate empirical work on the be-

haviour of teachers in four main areas: training; teachers' roles and professional relationships; the classroom and the communication structure; motivation and assessment of pupils. It has a particularly useful bibliography.

NIBLETT, W. R. (ed.), *How and Why do we Learn?*, Faber, 1965.
A collection of nine very wide-ranging essays on learning. Part One of the book contains contributions from six well-known educationists. Particularly pertinent is an excellent summary by Ben Morris entitled 'How does a group learn to work together?'. Part Two contains three very individual contributions by Stephen Potter, Richard Hoggart and Lord Caradon, and focuses attention on the learning experiences which occur after one's schooldays.

SWIFT, D. F. *Basic Readings in the Sociology of Education*, Routledge & Kegan Paul, 1970.
A volume containing eighteen essays divided into five major sections: sociology and education; the social animal; the school; the social environment of the educational institution; and the social functions of education. In particular, the articles by Argyle, Staines and Swift are highly relevant to interaction processes in school. There are useful introductions to each section and a comprehensive bibliography. (The book itself is a companion volume to *The Sociology of Education*, by D. F. Swift, Routledge & Kegan Paul, 1969.)

B. *Social-Psychology and Child Development (general)*
EVANS, E. D. (ed.), *Children, Readings in Behavior and*

Development, Holt, Rinehart & Winston, N.Y., 1968. One of the most outstanding modern books on child development, this volume is a compilation of articles reflecting various facets of research in the area and is a convenient source of much original and seminal writing. Each article contains detailed references and a linking 'orientation' passage by the editor. Child rearing, motivation, cognition and social expectation form major sections of the book.

ELKIND, D., *Children and Adolescents*, Oxford University Press, N.Y., 1970.
Nine essays which interpret Piaget's theory and findings on the development of children's thinking and attempt to relate the implications of Piaget's work to current educational theory and practice.

KRECH, D., CRUTCHFIELD, R. S., and BALLACHEY, E. L., *Individual in Society*, McGraw-Hill, N.Y., 1962.
This is a wide-ranging, coherent and highly readable introduction to social-psychology. The main unit of analysis is the interpersonal behaviour event and the work itself is organized into four sections: basic psychological factors, attitudes, the social and cultural habitat and groups, organizations and the individual. It contains one of the most comprehensive bibliographies on the subject.

LEWIS, M. M., *Language, Thought and Personality in Infancy and Childhood*, Harrap, 1963.
Possibly one of the most important of Lewis's many books; this provides ordered and coherent instruction on the subject of children's language development and their concomitant intellectual and social growth.